A WWII SECRET

GLENN P. LARSON AND THE U-505

Beverly Larson Christensen

HELLGATE PRESS   ASHLAND, OR

©2022 Bev Christensen. All rights reserved. No part of this publication may be reproduced or used in any form or by any means, graphic, electronic or mechanical, including photocopying, recording, taping, or information and retrieval systems without written permission of the publisher.

Published by:
Hellgate Press (an imprint of L&R Publishing, LLC)
PO Box 3531
Ashland, OR 97520
hellgatepress.com
email: sales@hellgatepress.com
Interior design: Sasha Kincaid
Cover design: Shirley Larson Gniffke (front), L. Redding (back)
.
ISBN: 978-1-954163-31-7
Printed and bound in the United States of America
First edition 10 9 8 7 6 5 4 3 2 1

This book is dedicated to my parents, Glenn Peter and Clara Larson, and all members of the Greatest Generation

"Uncommon valor was a common virtue."
- Fleet Admiral Chester W. Nimitz, March 17, 1945.

"Be strong and courageous. Do not be afraid; do not be discouraged, for the LORD your God will be with you wherever you go."
- Joshua 1:9

"Courage is being scared to death, but saddling up anyway."
- John Wayne.

CONTENTS

ACKNOWLEDGMENTS

MY DEEP THANKS TO THOSE WHO have helped and encouraged me in writing this book. It is the story of my father's World War II navy adventure, including the hunt for *U-505*. After 12 years of research, interviews, planning, procrastination, and collaboration, it has finally become a reality.

Thank you to my mother, Clara, who turned 97 years old on May 9, 2021. She contributed her recollections as it is her story also. Dad's letters to Mom were also an important source, and my cousin, Linda Larson Engelman, provided me with her father, Duane Larson's, WWII letters to Uncle Martin. A special thank you to Julian Austin, 96, for corresponding with me about his first hand account of the *U-505* story. Thank you to the late Don Baker, *Guadalcanal* crew member, who I met in 2009 in Chicago at the 65th Reunion of the *U-505* capture. At the banquet, my mother and I sat at a table for four and visited with Don and another veteran beside the submarine. Thank you to his wife, Sue, for graciously allowing me to share select portions of his writing. Also, much gratitude is owed to the late Captain Daniel Gallery for the books that he wrote about the USS *Guadalcanal* and the *U-505*.

A special thank you to my sister, Shirley Larson Gniffke, for creating the cover. Several people have helped with editing: Julie Ingman Johnson, Cindy Nasset Rogers, Cathy Langemo, William Gay, Julie Eikamp, Kevin Carvel, and Dr. C. Herbert Gilliland. Thank you to those who shared stories: my mother Clara, Alton Ivey, Kasper Binstock, Avis Rutherford, Harold Bach, Richard DeMarco, Duane Larson, Lee Soehren, and others.

Thank you to all the encouragers, including Bob Schow, Lina Lamsters, Cindy Rogers, Deloris Helm, our sons, my siblings, and many others. Finally, most of all, a big thank you to my husband, Steve Christensen, for his patience and encouragement. May God bless all of the above.

INTRODUCTION

WAR CHANGES EVERYONE. IN JULY 1944, 900 men stood in formation as U.S. Navy Captain Daniel V. Gallery ordered everyone on the USS *Guadalcanal* to keep their recent event a secret. They could tell no one, but no one, about what had just happened on this cruise- not even wives, parents, or siblings. Gallery instructed the Commanders of the five Destroyer Escorts to also notify the 1,000 men on their ships in this Anti-submarine Warfare Task Group with the same warning.

A young North Dakota farm boy, Glenn Peter Larson, of Regent, was among those bursting with the best story of his life, but he and the rest kept the secret until Germany surrendered in 1945.

Glenn Peter Larson

CHAPTER 1

The Shakedown Cruise: Training for Battle

USS Guadalcanal *aircraft carrier*

ON OCTOBER 15, 1943, THE MEN of the newly commissioned USS *Guadalcanal* escort aircraft carrier completed preparations with a series of drills and loaded provisions. The ship left Astoria, Oregon, and headed down the Columbia River to the famous Columbia Bar, where the river meets the Pacific, creating huge waves. Heavy seas pounded the ship during her maiden voyage, and she pitched and rolled as they headed north toward Bremerton, Washington.

The ship's commanding officer, Captain Daniel Gallery, noted:

> *"That first night at sea, my farmer boys received a tough initiation into the realm of Neptune. We crossed the bar of the Columbia River on the*

tail end of a northwest gale. The bar was breaking, and white-capped rollers swept in before the wind, which was blowing great guns. The old girl started chomping at the bit as soon as she stuck her nose into it, and immediately proved that she knew how to heave and roll and pitch like a real ship. Before we had been out 15 minutes we were taking green water aboard on the flight deck, and I'm sure most of my lads bitterly regretted that they hadn't joined the Army."

As one sailor recalled years later, *"The ship went up and down, but my stomach just went up."* Glenn Larson, a 21-year old farm boy from the western North Dakota prairies, suffered sea sickness like many others on the cruise but soon developed his sea legs.

That first night, the crew was alarmed by the noise created when the thin plates between the hangar deck and the flight deck "oil canned" or buckled, on every pitch of the *Guadalcanal*. The plates would spring in when they were over the back of a wave and in tension and then spring out when they got in the lowest point or trough. The flexing metal caused a thunderous booming that reverberated throughout the ship and made them wonder if she would break in two.

In his book, *My Navy Career,* former *Guadalcanal* crewman, Howard Sherer, recalled, *"The ship took a heavy beating and, that night, a forward lookout was washed overboard and could not be found."*

Captain Gallery reported:

> *"There is one word which makes everyone's blood run cold when it rings through a ship. The cry is, "Man overboard!" On a dark night, it strikes a chill into every heart on the ship, but it hits the skipper harder than anyone else. He knows that what he does in the next five minutes will determine whether his man is recovered or lost. We heard the cry once on the Guadalcanal early in our career, when a green sea lifted one of our lookouts out of his station at the forward end of the flight deck and carried him overboard.*
>
> *I did everything I could think of that night, but it wasn't good enough.*

I couldn't find our man. Everyone in the ship knows that looking for a man in the water on a black night with a rough sea running is practically hopeless, and that a man can only survive for about 10 minutes at most in near-freezing water, but even so you hate yourself when you give the order to resume course and leave the spot. It's like abandoning the search for a lost child."

Captain Daniel V. Gallery, born on July 10, 1901, in Chicago, was appointed to the US Naval Academy in Annapolis, Maryland, in 1917. In 1927, he volunteered for naval air and received flight training at Pensacola, Florida's Naval Air Station. He flew seaplanes, torpedo planes, and amphibians, eventually winning third place in the National Air Races. He was assigned as the Naval Attache at the US Embassy in Great Britain. In 1941, shortly after WW II began, he was appointed commander of a patrol plane detachment in Reykjavik, Iceland, assigned to guarding passing ship convoys against German U-boats. Captain Gallery received a Bronze Star for his aerial fighting against German U-boat submarines. But the detachment's patrol range over the Atlantic was limited by the amount of fuel the planes could carry.

It became apparent that convoys crossing the Atlantic would have to be protected by aircraft carriers, if they were going to survive. U-Boat Hunter-Killer Groups were formed, with flanking escort destroyers positioned to protect the carriers. One of these task groups was formed around Captain Gallery's new carrier, the USS *Guadalcanal*.

After learning the maneuvering characteristics of the ship, Gallery returned the *Guadalcanal* to the Puget Sound Navy Yard, in Bremerton, Washington. A flat-bottomed barge pulled alongside her and delivered ammunition to the deck force. The all-hands crew hoisted cargo nets full of bombs out of the barge, hauled them over the deck and moved them below late into the night as the ship's disc jockey played "Praise the Lord and Pass the Ammunition."

CHAPTER 2

Before the Shakedown Cruise
Pre-Commissioning School

As THE AIRCRAFT CARRIER WAS BEING prepared, Captain Gallery's crew, coming from cities, small towns and farms around the country, assembled. Before boarding their ship, the crew got about six weeks' training at Bremerton. Most of the crew members were just out of boot camp and here, the men learned some of the basic facts of life about ships in general. Glenn and his friend, Randall J. Novak, were a little ahead of the game after attending a Navy training school in Iowa.

Here at Bremerton, the men studied the plans of the ship and many of the actual machines they would have to operate. They were organized into 13 ship crew divisions and started to get acquainted with their officers. The course's final week was a cruise in Puget Sound on the *Casablanca*. Like most of the new sailors, this was the first voyage on saltwater for Glenn and Randall.

Surviving crew members of some of the large U.S. carriers that were sunk at sea early in the war were now split up among the crews of the smaller escort carriers. In many cases, they were the only experienced sailors in the new crews, including the USS *Guadalcanal's*. The young men learned quickly how to operate the machinery which included the guns, radar, boilers and engines.

As Electrician Mates, Glenn and Randall served under the ship's Chief Electrician, S.S. Shepard. Electrician's Mates are petty officers who maintain and repair all electrical equipment on board. The equipment was quite varied and included such things as motors, generators, battery chargers, telephone systems, signal systems, electrical controls, power distribution systems, and lighting systems.

All of *Guadalcanal's* crew went through the Navy's Fire Fighting School at Bremerton. Run by professional firemen, the school taught the men how to fight fires all day long. They set fires to full-scale models of engine rooms, hangar decks, and other parts of a model ship. The students learned all of the newest fire fighting techniques and equipment, and how to rescue trapped people, snuff out the fire, and enter a blazing compartment using a fog nozzle as a shield.

Captain Gallery wouldn't ask his boys to do anything that he wouldn't do himself. He wrote:

> *"For the week you were in the school, you were just one jump ahead of being fried alive. They would put you in the far end of a gasoline-drenched compartment, light the thing off, and leave you to your own devices. The only way you could get out of there was to drive the fire out ahead of you, or get dragged out by the boys in the asbestos suits who watched through peepholes from the outside, ready to rush in, in case you hadn't studied your lesson properly and passed out...This training which the boys got at the Fire Fighting School paid off in a big way later."*

The ship's captain also went through the school. He recalled:

> *"They put me in places the Devil himself would have squawked about the heat and would have gotten the hell out of there. Time and time again, the only sensible thing to do was to throw that damned hose away and run.*
>
> *The only trouble was they, my shoe crew, were right there watching me.... So I just had to sweat it out, hoping that the boys in the asbestos suits would step in if necessary."*

Captain Gallery's crew respected him for that.

The sailors also had instructions on seamanship, swimming, airplane and ship identification, and physical fitness training. After Pre-Commissioning School, Glenn was granted two weeks' leave from the Navy.

Heading east, the train rumbled through the Rocky Mountains and across the Great Plains. On the home farm at Regent, the wheat harvest was in full swing.

It felt good to be home again.

CHAPTER 3

Prarie Roots

GLENN LARSON'S STORY BEGAN BACK IN Regent, North Dakota, a small farming community. He was delivered by Doc Hill just before midnight on September 12, 1922. Raymond, his Danish father, had arrived in the Regent area at the age of 16 to farm with his father, James Peter Larson, in 1906. Glenn's Grandpa James only stayed on the farm one year, and then moved to Mott, North Dakota, where he took a job at the Equity Elevator.

Before the village of Regent was established in 1910, Raymond rode his horse across the prairie over the present town site and he observed prairie dogs, coyotes, and three wolves on his way to Buffalo Butte.

Glenn's mother, Lillie, was the daughter of a Norwegian immigrant who moved his family west from North Dakota's Red River Valley in 1911. Robert

Clara Paulsen, Russell, Raymond & James Peter Larson

An early view of Regent, North Dakota

Schow opened a blacksmith shop in the new village established by the Milwaukee Railroad, where he operated a machine shop, blacksmith shop, and auto livery.

Once Glenn was born, the family, with two older brothers, Duane and Wayne, was complete.

Glenn's parents, Raymond and Lillie, June 15, 1915

In the years before Glenn's birth, Lillie's parents, Robert and Minnie Schow, of Regent, made frequent visits to Raymond and Lillie's farm, two miles east of town, to see their little grandsons. While en route to one of those family visits, tragedy struck one evening. It was November 11, 1920.

Lillie's sixteen-year-old brother, Robbie, was driving his parents' car when they approached the railroad tracks. The evening train was in sight. Robert told his son, Robbie, to hurry across the tracks so they could avoid a wait at the crossing. Robbie obeyed. The freight train struck the vehicle.

Robert, only 55 years old, was thrown under the train engine and killed instantly. The train continued moving, pushing the car forward until it came to a complete stop a short distance from the Regent Depot. Minnie's right arm sustained multiple fractures and, although Robbie wasn't injured physically, he was no doubt emotionally traumatized by the event for many years to come.

Robert Schow's funeral was a sad day for the family and the little village. A large crowd gathered at the Lutheran church, and he was buried beside his son, Karl, who died in 1916 when he was twelve years old. Robert, a blacksmith, had lovingly hand-forged and installed a chain-link fence around the Schow plot in the Regent Cemetery a few years prior in memory of their son, Karl. That chain fence remains to this day on the western edge of the Regent cemetery.

Two years later, Glenn was delivered at home by Dr. S.W. Hill, who had arrived in Regent in 1911 from the coal-mining region of West Virginia. His birth brought some joy to the grieving family. Duane and Wayne were so excited about their baby brother that they burst into the bedroom where Lillie was nursing the newborn. An excited six-year-old, Duane, tossed a toad on the bed and proudly declared with a smile, "Here's Andy," his prized toad. Raymond laughed and shared that story for years.

Like green grass after a warm summer rain, the Larson boys grew quickly in the wide-open prairie spaces. All three attended a country schoolhouse one mile north of their farmstead. The little white school house, Mauzey #1, stood like a sentinel on the prairie, with Black Butte looming in the background to the north-west. The schoolyard had two outdoor privies, better known as outhouses. A merry-go-round, teeter-totter, and metal

Lillie's parents, Robert and Minnie (Noben) Schow. Robert came from Gardner, ND

swing set were nearby for students to wear off extra energy at recess. A horse barn stood nearby where Glenn sometimes kept his pony after he arrived at school.

There was no school water well, so every week a different farm family was assigned the task of bringing drinking water. It was then poured into a large stoneware crock with a spigot, which was kept on a table in the school entry.

Periodically, some of the boys would sneak some of this precious water at recess and attempt to drown pocket gophers. (These pests can destroy crops and back then gopher hunters were instructed to bring gopher tails to their local township clerks, who would fill out the necessary paperwork and pay them the bounty of one cent per tail.)

One day, the teacher caught Glenn in this mischief, and she made him stay after school as punishment. Alton Ivey, a younger student, recalled with a chuckle that, as he picked up his lunch box to go home, Glenn said, "What about Alton?" To his dismay, he too, had to stay inside as the other students were dismissed.

Winter snow provided fun outdoor activities at recess including playing a game of Fox and Geese, snowball fights, making forts or building a snowman. Every winter brought at least one blizzard, and the Larson boys were delighted to be kept home from school while the storm raged. Since outdoor farm chores, such as milking the cows, still had to be done, the boys helped as able. After the storm subsided, the landscape was transformed into a winter wonderland with newly formed snow drifts so high that they beckoned the boys to dig tunnels and caves. Glenn's best friend in country school was J. Slade DeLaney, who also had a prestigious war career. He went on to earn his wings in 1944 during WWII. He served as a multi-engine pilot with the Manhattan Project, the code name for the development of the first atomic bombs.

While growing up, Glenn's brothers would sometimes take him along to the Cannonball River on a sultry summer day. It flowed past Regent and the Larson farm, winding its way through the beautiful prairie grass to the Missouri River. Here, the boys enjoyed swimming and horseplay with their friends.

One warm day, after Glenn had learned to swim, he dove in. To his shock, his head stuck in the mud at the bottom of the river. He frantically struggled to free himself and learned a valuable lesson about diving.

Glenn's lifelong love of horses was reflected in his favorite childhood book, *Black Beauty*. Occasionally when he was a child, his father would help him put

Glenn and his pony, Ben

Brothers Wayne, Glenn and Duane Larson

a little harness on his pony, Ben, and attach a small cart. He is hauling some corn in the photo.

When the drought of the Dirty Thirties hit, life became more difficult. Temperatures soared above 100 degrees for multiple days, and the grass and crops dried up. Swarms of grasshoppers flew in on the wind and devoured anything that looked faintly green. The extreme drought caused cattle and sheep to starve, and with no crops to sell, many farm boys sought jobs elsewhere. Glenn's brother, Wayne, left the farm and took a job as an orderly at St. Paul Ramsey Hospital in St. Paul, Minnesota.

In 1933, the third year of the severe economic depression, President Franklin Roosevelt created the Civilian Conservation Corps or CCC program to provide jobs for unemployed young men between ages 18 and 25. They received $30 in payment per month, plus room and board.

In 1934, when Glenn was 11 years old, a Hettinger County CCC project began to build a dam on Spring Creek near Larson's farmyard. His father, Raymond,signed an easement to allow a low area of his land to be flooded by water behind the dam. Using one tractor and several teams of horses, the CCC constructed a concrete, earth-filled dam to raise the water level on Spring Creek by 12 feet to form Larson Lake in a dry lowland area to the south.

Glenn's oldest brother, Duane, age 17, and a neighbor, Tony Binstock, were hired, but lived at home. Using their own teams of horses, they joined the CCC men who traveled from their camp at New England, North Dakota, every morning.

Three more years of drought followed the completion of the dam. Glenn recalled that one afternoon rain clouds appeared and then precious drops of rain finally began to fall. It continued through the night, pelting the window panes and roof, answering everyone's prayers.

The next morning, Glenn rushed to the upstairs hall window, where he observed with delight a lake had formed overnight. Now the Regent area had a lake in which to swim and cool off after a hard day's work. Little did Glenn know that his swimming skills would one day enable him to pass the required Navy swimming test.

Glenn enjoyed working on the farm, and one of his duties was to cultivate the young corn plants. The prairie was filled with songs of meadowlarks and blackbirds, which followed behind the cultivator to eat worms and insects in the freshly dug up soil. Sometimes, while cultivating, Glenn said he would daydream about sailing the high seas someday.

Glenn, Duane, Raymond and Wayne Larson

All three boys attended high school in Regent. Raymond promised the boys a gold watch if they didn't smoke during their formative years. Duane and Wayne received a gold watch upon graduation from high school, but Glenn was caught smoking out behind the barn.

After his brother, Duane graduated, he went to work for his uncle, Martin Schow, near Stanton, North Dakota. Martin was a rancher and pioneer pilot who had built an airplane in 1927 and taught himself how to fly. Here Duane learned about aviation when he was not busy with chores.

While Glenn attended high school, war was escalating in Europe. Germany's Adolf Hitler invaded Poland in 1939, followed by Britain and France declaring war on Germany.

One of Glenn's schoolmates, Avis Trunkhill Rutherford, turned 95 on May 14, 2021. She recalled that Glenn was a lot of fun and always a daredevil in high school, especially with his motorcycle. His younger neighbor, Kasper Binstock, shared that sometimes Glenn took him along in his sidecar when he checked his fur trap line on the Cannonball River.

Glenn and his motocycle

Glenn before he enlisted in WWII

Glenn graduated from Regent High School in 1940 along with 16 other students. There was a sense of pride in growing up at Regent, and the community supported the youth with their positive values and sense of patriotism.

One summer, probably 1941, Glenn, and his good friend, Randall Novak, of Regent rode motorcycles to Sturgis, South Dakota in the Black Hills, a distance of about 180 miles. The first Sturgis Motorcycle Rally was held there in 1938 and has been held every year since except 1942 when gasoline was rationed.

CHAPTER 4

The World Situation

THE WAR IN THE ATLANTIC OCEAN began on September 3, 1939, when Britain announced a naval blockade of Germany. Germany ordered a counter-blockade of the Allies eight days later to prevent food and war materials from reaching Britain and France.

In April 1940, a month before Glenn graduated from high school, Germany invaded Denmark and Norway. Denmark surrendered almost immediately, and Norway fell in June. As a result, Britain's Prime Minister, Arthur Neville Chamberlain, who favored appeasing Hitler, was succeeded by Winston Churchill. Germany continued to bulldoze its way into Holland, Belgium, Luxembourg, and France. Italy's Mussolini joined Germany's side that June.

In the fall of 1940, Germany, Japan, and Italy joined together and signed the Axis Pact. Winston Churchill's Britain, alone, kept democracy alive during the Battle of Britain in September 1940.

In January 1941, Glenn's brother, Wayne, joined the U.S. Army at Fort Snelling, Minnesota. He was sent to California, where he served in radio and wire communications as a Staff Sergeant with the 747th Anti-aircraft Artillery Automatic Weapons Battalion. Sergeant Wayne Larson was a Communications Chief for the duration of the war.

The first woman to enlist was Mildred Bowers, the daughter of Regent's banker, Harold and Claribel (Westaby) Bowers. She graduated from Evanston, Illinois, School of Nursing, joined the Army Nurses Corps, and was commissioned a Lieutenant. Mildred married James L. Smith of Stockton, in San Francisco on May 4, 1942. (Mott Press, May 14, 1942) He became an Army Air Corps bomber pilot on missions over Japan."

Wayne, Raymond, Duane, Lillie and Glenn, 1941

During this time, German battleships were busy sinking supply ships crossing the Atlantic in convoys. It was Churchill's outstanding leadership that enabled British forces to gradually fight back against the Axis. Germany had two of the biggest ships in the Atlantic, the *Bismarck*, and the *Tirpitz*. On May 24, 1941, the *Bismarck* sunk the British battle cruiser *Hood*, and only three of its 1,419 crewmen escaped. Three days later, the British sank the *Bismarck*. The *Tirpitz* never fired at an enemy ship, but spent most of World War II in German-occupied ports of Norway, where her presence was a significant threat. Germany then turned to U-boat warfare against Allied shipping.

The next month, June 1941, Hitler's Axis forces betrayed Stalin by invading the Soviet Union. The retreating Russians destroyed food supplies, factories, dams, and railroads ahead of the advancing Germans to ensure the Germans wouldn't have access to these things. As a result, the Germans ran out of winter supplies and the weather was bitterly cold. However, these actions also affected the Russians, who also suffered greatly during these hard times.

After conferring aboard a warship in the Atlantic, Churchill and Roosevelt issued the *Atlantic Charter* on August 14, 1941. It declared that the United States and Britain sought no territory, and it proclaimed the right of all peoples to choose their own form of government and have no boundary changes imposed on them. It declared the right of all to freedom at home and at sea.

Britain's Prime Minister Churchill later wrote that the only thing that really frightened him during the war was the steadily mounting tonnage lost to "*the U-boat peril.*"

CHAPTER 5

Hitler and His German U-Boats

MEANWHILE, IN GERMANY, ON AUGUST 26, 1941, the *U-505* submarine was commissioned at Hamburg, Germany. It was 252-feet long, displaced 1,100 tons when loaded, and carried a crew of four officers and 56 men. WW II submarines were actually a surface craft that could operate submerged when necessary for short periods of time. It could go down to 500 to 600 feet and had two powerful diesel engines, a pair of heavy electric motors, many pumps, and a huge storage battery. *U-505* carried twenty-one torpedoes. The pressure hull was a rigid steel cylinder that contained all the machinery, essential equipment, and living spaces.

A model like U-505, a type IXC German U-boat

Attached to the outside of the pressure hull were large ballast tanks. They were actually buoyancy tanks; when empty, they kept the heavy pressure hull afloat. They had sea valves in the bottom and air valves on the top. When both were opened to allow seawater to flow in, air was forced out of the top vents, which allowed the submarine to sink.

The same day the *U-505* was launched and the *Atlantic Charter* was signed, Glenn's brother, Duane, entered the Army Air Corps at Ft. Snelling in St. Paul, Minnesota.

The following month, in September 1941, German forces blockaded St. Petersburg (Leningrad), Russia. The siege lasted 872 days, almost two and a half years. Ending January 27, 1944, it was one of the longest, most destructive, and lethal sieges of a major city in modern history. More than one million civilians were killed, mostly from starvation, and the beautiful Baltic port city, with more than 50 imperial mansions and palaces built during Peter the Great's reign, became largely depopulated.

CHAPTER 6

Pearl Harbor

ON SUNDAY, DECEMBER 7, 1941, SEEMINGLY out of nowhere, Japanese carrier attack planes and bombers, supported by fighters, surprise attacked Pearl Harbor in two waves. Glenn's future brother-in-law, Dick Jordan, was serving on the USS *Indianapolis* at that time. He was safe on shore at Pearl Harbor when the Japanese bombs struck, but his ship was at sea, executing morning exercises. The *Indianapolis*, upon receiving news of the attack, immediately joined Task Force 12 and searched for Japanese carriers reportedly still in the vicinity.

The United States declared war on Japan the next day, and President Franklin Roosevelt's address included his famous words, "*A date which will live in infamy.*"

Four days later, on December 11, Germany and Japan declared war on the United States. Following the Japanese attack at Pearl Harbor, millions of American men entered the United States military by both volunteering and conscription. By the end of 1941, Japan had almost total command of the entire Southeast Asia region.

By May 1942, Wayne was studying radio in San Francisco, and Duane, stationed in Georgia, passed his pilot's test. According to the *Mott Pioneer Press* report, "*Seems only yesterday these two Larsons were riding around on their motorcycle.*"

That same month, the advancing Japanese Imperial Navy attempted to take all of New Guinea and the Solomon Islands. The Battle of the Coral Sea was the first of the Pacific Ocean War's six battles between opposing aircraft carriers and their forces. Glenn's future brother-in-law, Dick Jordan, was now aboard the USS *Lexington*, which was hit by a Kamikaze dive bomber and torpedoes. Leaking aviation fuel ignited and exploded. Jordan and the rest of *Lexington's* crew were rescued from their burning ship by a nearby destroyer, and the ship was scuttled to prevent her capture. This was a severe loss for the U.S. Navy as the *Lexington* was one of its largest carriers.

The United States' other aircraft carrier, the USS *Yorktown*, was damaged, but quickly repaired at Pearl Harbor before it was rushed into the Battle of Midway (June 4-6, 1942). Japan's ships outnumbered the American forces by nearly four to one, but the U.S. had cracked Japan's secret codes and knew about Admiral Yamamoto's plans. The Battle of Midway was one of the most decisive victories in United States history and a turning point in the Pacific War. That same month Dwight D. Eisenhower assumed total command of the United States Army in Europe.

CHAPTER 7

Operation Drumbeat

HITLER'S U-BOAT, *U-123*, SLOWLY CREPT OUT of the heavily fortified cement bunkers at the German U-boat headquarters, in Lorient, France on December 23, 1941. Submerged, she could make only 7.3 knots, but once surfaced, the diving boat could cruise and fight like a torpedo boat. Diesel engine power allowed *U-123* to travel at a maximum speed of 18 1/4 knots on the surface, which was faster than merchantmen and some escort vessels. At 12 knots she could travel over 8,700 nautical miles without refueling. When submerged and running on her electric motors, the batteries would run out of power after only 64 miles. To fully recharge the batteries the U-boat had to run its diesels on the surface for seven hours.

When Japan surprise attacked Pearl Harbor on December 7, 1941, Hitler was stunned. Just six months prior, Germany had invaded the Soviet Union, and by December 2 they were just north of Moscow. In the freezing Russian winter, more than 4.3 million German soldiers were battling against 3.3 million Soviet troops. The largest military operation in world history was putting a serious strain on Germany's armed forces.At the same time, Hitler was also aware that the British and Americans had created military plans to wage war together against Germany. So just four days after the attack on Pearl Harbor, he declared war on the United States.

This began the second phase of the Battle of the Atlantic, for which the United States Navy was not adequately prepared. Starting in 1939, Germany attempted to stop Britain's imports of food and raw materials. When the war began in Europe, the United States maintained neutrality while increasing its fleet. President Franklin Roosevelt pushed to assist Britain and loaned them old destroyers in exchange for the use of British bases in the Western

Hemisphere. In 1941 the United States' Forces began occupying bases in Greenland and Iceland.

Before France fell to Germany in June 1940, the U-boats had to sail from ports on the Baltic or North Sea. They had to pass through heavily defended waters north of the British Isles to reach the Atlantic Ocean. Lorient, France, and its naval base was captured by the Germans on June 21, 1940, without a shot fired. After capturing France's naval bases, Hitler ordered the construction of a massive U-boat bunker along the Saint-Nazaire waterfront at Lorient. It consisted of a 980 feet long reinforced concrete and steel structure. The bunker contained fourteen separate U-boat pens, eight which could hold a single U-boat and six that were wide enough for two U-boats. The roof of the structure consisted of twenty-eight feet of concrete and steel reinforcements that were bomb-proof in case of enemy air attacks.

Germany's submariners were an esteemed group of men and the most elite fighting force in their navy. They received higher pay than the surface naval crews, and elaborate ceremonies were held at both their send-off and return to base. Life, however, was hard inside the small, confined areas in the submarines, and their missions could be for extended periods of time, weeks or even months. The crew received three hot meals a day and "hot bunks" for sleeping on a rotating basis, due to the limited space. Sheets were changed and washed when they returned to base, as there was no laundry service on the boats. The crew consisted of about fifty men working together in close physical contact in the narrow confines of the U-boat's steel hull. It was a stressful and inhospitable environment. The Control room, which occupied the midship space directly below the conning tower, was the nerve center of the U-boat.

Karl Donitz, Hitler's senior submarine officer, made plans for the later part of 1941 for a swift and coordinated attack on the eastern seaboard of the United States. For this plan he needed U-boats that were capable of cruising across the Atlantic, so he requested twelve type IX boats.

Eight of Hitler's U-boats had been assigned to the Baltic area to protect the nautical flank of Army Group North, and six U-boats were dispatched to Norway to attack Soviet shipping. By December 10, 86 U-boats were either operating in the eastern Mediterranean and its approaches to the Strait of

Gibraltar or on standby to relieve others on patrol. So, only five operational Type IX boats were actually available for what became known as Operation Drumbeat. These U-boats set sail around Christmas 1941 for the two-week journey west to American waters. They were now able to wage unrestricted submarine warfare.

Admiral Ernest J. King was appointed Commander-in-Chief of the United States Fleet two days before New Year's Eve 1941. Prior to that he was commander of the Atlantic Fleet, and he knew that the East coast warships and crews were strained due to the dire demand for ships in the Pacific against Japan. The Atlantic Fleet had only five battleships, two aircraft carriers and fourteen cruisers operating against the Germans by the end of January 1942. Aware of the shortage, President Roosevelt pledged a crash program to build 2,250 new tankers, freighters and bulk carriers within the next two years. At the time, American defenses along the East coast were almost nonexistent.

Meanwhile, *U-123*, under Captain Reinhard Hardegen, and four other U-boats were crossing the Atlantic, each headed to a separate operational area. One night, *U-123*'s lookout man discovered an alarming narrow black silhouette visible against the night sky. It turned out to be another surfaced submarine. The signalman flashed the December code with his light and Captain Hardegen ordered his men to their battle stations. The other U-boat flashed back that it was *UA* returning to Lorient, France, from patrol off South Africa. They were currently carrying fifty extra men that they had rescued at sea after *Python*, a German refueling and supply ship, was sunk by a British cruiser. Hardegen sent back the message, "Well Done. Great seamanship. Happy Christmas," as *UA* disappeared from view into the dark night.

To celebrate Christmas, Captain Hardegen had small Christmas trees delivered to every compartment on the submarine. The largest tree was set up in the Control room and decorated with electric lights by the boat's electricians.

The captain allotted a measure of red wine punch to each man, which they slowly savored. They knew it would be their last drink for several weeks. The captain read the Nativity story from Luke, which was followed by a holiday meal. Presents from German children were distributed as well as the much anticipated mail. The men's hearts were most touched by the Christmas greetings from their family and friends back home. Then they gathered around the lighted Christmas tree and a couple men took turns playing music on an accordion. That night, as they sang "Silent Night, Holy Night" in German, both the Atlantic and Mediterranean theaters were quiet and peaceful for the moment.

Steadily, the wolf pack of *U-123* and four other longer-range Type IX U-boats headed for the North American coast. Meanwhile, in Washington, President Roosevelt and Prime Minister Churchill created the Joint Declaration of the United Nations, which they signed on January 1, 1942. Ultimately, 24 other nations signed it, including the Soviet Union and China, pledging to fight until the Axis was defeated.

Hitler's Admiral Donitz was able to send and receive communications between his headquarters, in Lorient, France and the U-boats at sea. At the same time, code breakers at Berlin intercepted and decrypted messages between the Royal Navy's Command in Liverpool and convoy escort groups at sea. By early 1942, both the Germans and Allies were reading each others naval communications without the other side's awareness.

The German U-boat Force utilized the M3 naval Enigma machine to send its coded messages. A sequence of eight Enigma rotors were changed every other day to make it more complex. Yet, by January 1942, the British were able to read the contents of the messages between the supreme commander of the German Navy's U-Boat Arm, and the U-boats. On January 12, British intelligence provided the United States and Canadian Navies with an explicit and accurate warning of a wide-spread and imminent attack by German U-boats against east coast shipping. Astonishingly, the Americans did nothing!

By January 13, all the U-boats were to be in position along the East Coast to begin their attacks simultaneously. Two days prior, *U-123 sank* the British freighter *SS Cyclops* east of Boston. It had been on its way to the New York Harbor. Donitz ordered the U-boats to stay submerged during the day and ambush merchant ships during the darkness of night. Unfortunately, at this time the United States' Atlantic Fleet destroyer force was spread out across the Atlantic from Iceland to the coast of Brazil. The few destroyers left on the East coast were committed to escort a large troop convoy from New York to Northern Ireland.

The East Coast's air defense arm was even more pathetic at that time and was unable to mount quick-reaction flights in response to U-boat sightings. Furthermore, the American coast was not darkened as in Europe, but lit up like a Christmas tree at night. Allied ships along the coast were made completely visible by the light coming from the coast, and their silhouettes made them easy targets for the U-boats.

Germany's *U-123* made the first attack of the day on January 14, 1942, as it sank a Norwegian tanker within sight of Long Island before it entered New York Harbor. It also sank a British tanker off Sandy Hook. The sinking was not reported in the newspapers as the Navy wanted to suppress the negative war news from the public.

The first wave of Germany's Operation Drumbeat proceeded to sink 25 ships with the loss of hundreds of Allied lives and more than 100,000 tons of supplies. Low on fuel, the U-boats ended operations off the coast of America on February 6 and headed for home. Upon return to their French base they were met with the usual welcoming bands, flowers, girls and homecoming perks.

After the initial success, Donitz ordered a second wave of attacks. This group included the mid-range submarines which were enhanced to make the trip. Some of the submarines' drinking water reservoirs were even used to carry diesel fuel. According to Ed Offey's *The Burning Shore*, on February 1, Vice Admiral Karl Donitz deployed a new encryption machine on U-boats, which delayed the British and Americans from timely U-boat intelligence for most of 1942. In February 1942, 16 U-boats patrolled the North American waters from Nova Scotia to eastern Venezuela. This time period was known as the "The Second Happy Time," for the U-boat crews, as they sank thirty-five Allied merchant ships and one warship. Their favorite targets in the Caribbean were Allied oil tankers.

On March 7, Admiral King received a letter from the British Ministry of War Transport in Canada suggesting that the United States might do as the British had done at Dunkirk. This letter encouraged the United States to utilize a volunteer fleet of private small watercraft to assist the Navy with patrol and rescue. Under King's direction, Admiral Andrews ordered Naval District commandants to purchase private power craft under 100 feet.

Eventually, 143 suitable watercraft armed with .50-caliber machine guns were acquired, and manned by the Coast Guard.

A third wave of attacks off North America's eastern coastlines was expected in March. This was due to a pattern of ship losses and Bletchley Park's isolated HF/DF (high frequency radio direction finder) intercepts, which indicated that at least ten U-boats were moving westward across the North Atlantic.

In late March, a new type of U-boat, known as a "milch (milk) cow," entered operational service. It was specifically designed to replenish the U-boats at sea with fuel and food supplies. It carried 720 tons of diesel fuel, 34 tons of lubricating oil, and ten tons of fresh water. Now Donitz was able to dispatch shorter range U-boats for up to 66 days.

By the end of March forty-seven Allied merchant ships and two warships had been sunk, and Admiral Andrews and the six naval districts were in a full-fledged panic. Some 45 percent of the overall 216 Allied merchant ships that were sunk by U-boats in North American coastal waters and the Caribbean between January and mid-April were British vessels. England sent Commander Rodger Winn to Washington, D.C. to plead with Admiral Ernest King to instigate a coastal convoy system and form a submarine tracking room. During April, according to the United States Navy Eastern Sea Frontier war diary, these areas were described as, "the most dangerous area for merchant shipping in the entire world." (*Operation Drumbeat*, p. 342)

Subsequently, Admiral King created a submarine tracking room and developed a plan with the Army to darken the coastline from Maine to the Florida Keys at night. The convoy system, though, took much longer to implement, due to the lack of destroyers. In the meantime, the Navy continued to withhold reporting of the coastal losses from the general public. Insurance companies stopped writing policies on merchant vessels, and engine room men on tankers were leaving the ships in large numbers.

In the spring of 1942, the United States Army Air Force was a fighting force in its infancy. The army's B-17 aircraft could patrol as far as six hundred miles offshore, while medium-range B-25 and B-26 bombers flew shorter circuits of up to several hundred miles. Daily patrols of two aircraft per operation started at Bangor, Maine; Westover Field, Massachusetts; Mitchel Field, New York; and Langley Field, Virginia. The underside of the bombers was painted black to prevent the U-boat look-outs from spotting the aircraft and crash-diving before an attack. The result was U-boat sightings and sinking jumped 30 percent.

Next, Admiral Andrews endorsed the idea of engaging the services of the Civil Air Patrol. They were private pilots with their own light airplanes who patrolled the coastal waters and forced the U-boats under water. The spotting planes made it difficult for them to operate on the surface, which prevented them from recharging their batteries.

Several hundred private aircraft were making scheduled patrol flights by late spring. The Army supplied the CAP planes with aviation fuel, but the pilots had to provide their own hangars and maintenance. According to *Operation Drumbeat*, p. 356, half of all the aircraft carried either two 100-pound demolition bombs or one 325-pound depth charge and a simple garage-built bombsight.

The Civilian Air Patrol flew in every kind of weather, even in the foulest conditions when military pilots were grounded. Although the pilots couldn't destroy any U-boats, they reported the boats' positions and forced U-boats underwater. They also helped locate lifeboats and rafts, leading to the rescue of 363 survivors from sunken merchant ships. The CAP aviators called in a total of 173 separate U-boat sightings and contributed significantly against Germany's U-boat attacks along the America coast in World War II. The pilots were commendable examples of civilian generosity and bravery during war and helped to eventually draw the U-boats' "Happy Time" to a close.

On May 14, 1942, seven escort warships departed Norfolk, Virginia, for Key West to accompany the nineteen merchant ships that made up Convoy KS500. Easy pickings by the U-boats were coming to an end. That same day Donitz briefed Hitler on the planned mine-laying campaign at coastal ports by *U-701* and two other U-boats. Captain Degen's *U-701* was loaded with fifteen TMB seabed mines in its five torpedo tubes and departed Lorient, France, for its three-week transit to the US east coast. During this time period, navy code breakers deciphered a planned Japanese attack at Midway in the Pacific Ocean. It positioned the aircraft carriers USS *Enterprise,* USS *Hornet, and* USS *Yorktown* for an ambush against four carriers.

Between June 4 and 7, the United States sank all four Japanese carriers and a cruiser and destroyed 248 carrier aircraft and their aircrews. America lost one carrier, the *Yorktown,* a destroyer and 150 aircraft. Victory was celebrated for the first time since the Pearl Harbor attack and gave America the offensive in the Pacific. Now the US Air Force moved the 396th Medium Bombardment Squadron and all fifteen of its A-29 Hudson bombers from the West Coast to eastern North Carolina to hunt for German U-boats.

Donitz was unaware that the Eastern Sea Frontier knew that several U-boats were on their way to the US East Coast to lay minefields. Patrols were increased, but the U-boats managed to lay forty-five German mines up and down the eastern seaboard. Many sank too deeply to detonate when ships passed overhead.

By July, increased air coverage and the use of convoys greatly decreased the sinking of Allied vessels. On June 21, 1942, Admiral King stated, "Escort is not just one way of handling the submarine menace: it is the *only* way that gives any promise of success" (*Operation Drumbeat*, p. 388). Unfortunately, in the previous six months more than half a million tons of shipping was sent to the bottom of the sea along the American coast. It was America's worst-ever defeat at sea, and its costliest. It was Germany's most successful sustained U-boat campaign in WWII, although the public had no way of knowing it.

During the last six months of 1942, Germany built 121 U-boats, and only 58 were sunk. Winston Churchill and President Roosevelt met at Casablanca in January 1943 and agreed that the defeat of the U-boat was the first priority in the battle for Europe.

By March 1943, the first Escort Carrier Group was organized, with four destroyers operating as a screen for the aircraft carrier. It carried high speed Grumman F4F-3 *Wildcat* and RBF-1 *Avenger* aircraft that followed radar and Huff-Duff bearings to bomb and strafe surfaced U-boats before they could completely submerge.

Eventually, eleven "Hunter-Killer" carrier groups operating in the Atlantic would become the great destroyer of Germany's U-boats.

Glenn Larson would be a member of one of the Hunter-Killer task groups.

Glenn Larson enlisted in the Navy in 1942

CHAPTER 8

Raymond's Battle

BACK AT THE FARM NEAR REGENT, North Dakota, the Larson brothers' father was fighting his own battle. He suffered a badly bruised body and broken ribs when his herd bull, Ferdinand, attacked him while he was driving his cattle out to pasture. The bull tossed Raymond to the ground after hitting him in the ribs and then trampled him before he could get up. Fortunately, Ferdinand had no horns, and Raymond was able to get up and walk away. He credited his dog with saving his life. (*Mott Pioneer Press*, June 18, 1942)

Glenn took over the bulk of the farm work that summer while his father healed from broken ribs and various contusions. His mother, Lillie, was also accustomed to doing outdoor chores, which including milking cows, separating cream, feeding calves, gardening, and taking care of the chickens. No doubt, she penned letters to Duane and Wayne when she could find the time and now had three family members in her prayers.

Did she know Glenn was contemplating the idea of signing up to serve Uncle Sam also? The Selective Service Act required all men between the age of 18 and 44 to register for the draft, but one could be deferred to support national health, safety, war production, agriculture occupation, or extreme hardship and privation to wife, child, or parent.

Glenn could have easily avoided service because he qualified in two of the areas, agriculture and privation to parent, but he chose to serve.

In the summer of 1942, the Regent community was shocked and saddened to learn from a Washington, D.C., report that a hometown lad, LaVern "Buster" Ulmer, was Missing in Action on August 18 in the Philippines. He enlisted in the US Army in December 1938 at Fort Lincoln and served in the Philippines three years. During the bombing on December 7, 1941, he was in the Hq. Squadron 24 at Clark Field, Pampamya. Fighting from one of the Bataan foxholes in the big battle, LaVern participated in major combat and did his part in repulsing the hordes of Japanese who time after time sought to conquer them. They finally succeeded when General MacArthur, short of men and ammunition, was forced to capitulate. Ulmer died in a Japanese prison camp and is remembered as a gallant American soldier.

CHAPTER 9

Glenn Enlists: Off to Boot Camp

By December 1942, Glenn's brother, Duane, was stationed at the U.S. Army Air Forces Training Detachment at Helena, Arkansas. He wrote:

> "I've got two hours of solo time now and 14 hours all together. In another four or five hours, I'll be getting a check from a check pilot. I hope there's a good angel in my cockpit then. My instructor and I were up above the clouds today. Boy was it pretty up there. We did four spins on the way down. They have washed out a bunch of our class already. If I can make it through the first check and keep from smashing up any equipment, I should make it through primary. We get about 60 hours here. Pretty soon we'll start with acrobatics, snap rolls, slow rolls, Immelmanns (roll-off-the-top turn maneuver), Chandelles (a maneuver where the pilot combines a 180 degree turn with a climb) and such stuff, provided we get that far. I have started instrument flying in the Link Trainer too."

By now Raymond had healed from the bull attack, and Glenn was eager to join his brothers in the war effort. In *Wild at Heart,* John Eldredge wrote:

> "Every man's soul longs for three things: a battle to fight, a beauty to rescue, and an adventure to live...A man needs a battle to fight, he needs a place for the warrior in him to come alive...to become truly masculine; it is hardwired into every man...a mission God made (him) for."

Initially, Glenn's parents opposed the idea of him enlisting. He was their last son and was needed on the farm. But through perseverance and persistence, Glenn convinced his father it was something he needed to do, and Raymond finally gave his permission, blessing, and signature as his guardian.

Glenn and his best friend, Randall Novak, signed up for the Navy at Mott, North Dakota. The local paper reported that the following young men from Regent, "Stanley Nelson, Glenn Larson, Randall Novak and Johnny Bambusch left Monday morning for Fargo to take their final examination before being inducted into the navy."

So on December 8, 1942, Lillie, with tears in her eyes, tightly hugged her last son goodbye as he boarded the train for Fargo. Her heart was breaking, but she tried her best not to show it. Lillie and Raymond were always very proud of their sons, but the agonizing thought of losing any one of them was hard to bear. Like most other parents, the Larsons became active prayer warriors for their sons' safe return.

In Fargo, the Medical Examiner noted that Glenn had a two-inch indented scar behind his right ear from a mastoid operation in 1928. For a moment, Glenn was six again, as he remembered the intense pain he had endured from the infection that started with an ear infection and progressed to his mastoid skull bone. This was before penicillin was available, and when Dr. Hill couldn't cure it, his parents took him to Bismarck. There, a surgeon removed part of the skull bone behind Glenn's ear, and the doctor instructed his mother to apply a purple medicine to the wound daily at home. During this procedure, Glenn's brother, Duane, remembered hearing his screams of pain all the way down at the barn. Fortunately, the treatment worked, and the boy recovered.

On December 11, 1942, Glenn was sworn into the US Navy at Fargo when he and Randall took the oath of enlistment, then boarded a train headed for Idaho. They stared out the window as the Northern Pacific wound its way west through the night, and wondered what lay ahead.

On December 15, Glenn and Randall arrived in Farragut, Idaho for boot camp training. There was no town there; just Farragut Naval Station, which was a 40,000-acre inland naval base. Because the United States feared a possible Japanese invasion, the camp was established more than 300 miles from the West Coast. It was located on the southern tip of Lake Pend Oreille

Glenn and friend Randall Novak of Regent, North Dakota

in the Coeur d'Alene Mountains of the Bitterroot Range. Between September 1942 and June 1946, almost 300,000 naval recruits received their boot camp training there.

The base's six training units were designed for 5,000 men each. The Farragut Naval Station was built in a great hurry, and many of the 776 buildings were constructed with green wood due to a scarce lumber supply. It became the second-largest naval training center in the world. And during this time period, it became Idaho's largest city. Glenn wondered, "What have I gotten myself into?"

As soon as new recruits arrived, they received their shots, a buzz haircut, their uniforms, a serial number, a seabag, and The Bluejackets' Manual. Sleeping gear consisted of a hammock with a mattress and covers, a pillow with two covers, and two blankets. When traveling, a sailor rolled up his mattress and sleeping gear inside his hammock and secured it to his seabag. He could sling this pack over his shoulder and march off with everything he owned.

Boot camp consisted of hours upon hours of physical fitness training as a unit, following commands and basic skills like marching, rifle range, manual of arms, gas mask drill, a rugged obstacle course, swimming, rowing, and seamanship classes. Basic training taught recruits to obey commands, stick together, and depend on each other as a unit.

To qualify for the Navy, a recruit was required to pass his swimming test. He had to be able to enter the water feet first from a platform the height of an aircraft carrier deck, swim the length of an Olympic size pool, and get out. Growing up on the prairie at Regent, Randall had never learned to swim and, in fact, was afraid of the water. Glenn later admitted that he assumed Randall's ID and took his swimming test for him, without any questions asked of him. Did the Navy know but look the other way, as all recruits were desperately needed to fill the demand on newly built warships?

The men of Company 157, Regiment 4, Battalion 16, U.S. Naval Training Station, Farragut, Idaho, under Basil Marella, Company Commander, had their group photo taken on February 2, 1943.

Glenn qualified in both marksmanship and swimming on February 12. His parents traveled to Farragut to attend his Boot Camp Graduation. Glenn and his fellow recruits marched in review in front of the commandant and his staff, and the band played while they went through their drill on Graduation Day.

On February 15, 1943, he boarded the train, along with Randall and fellow sailors, for their transfer journey to Ames, Iowa.

CHAPTER 10

Iowa State and The Battle of the Atlantic

THE U.S. NAVY HAD COLLABORATED WITH Iowa State College in Ames to create an Electrical Naval Training School on Iowa State's campus. Men were selected on the basis of their mechanical aptitude in qualifying examinations given to all Navy men at Navy enlistment centers (*The Iowa Engineer*, Oct. 1941, p. 5).

On February 21, 1943, Glenn and his fellow sailors began classes in Electricians Mate School. They attended classes on Gyro Compass, Amphibious Force, Fleet, Submarine, Interior Communication, Destroyer-Escort, Anti-Aircraft Protection, and Submarine Repair.

Two dormitory halls, Huges and Friley, with close to 350 separate rooms, were transformed as closely as possible to resemble ship's quarters. Room doors were removed, and the Navy provided double and triple decker bunks in the rooms. All floors were known as decks, the walls were referred to as bulkheads, the ceilings were called overheads, and all stairways were called ladders. There was also a brig for disciplining men and military time was established. These changes helped the men quickly prepare for the routines and vocabulary of ship life.

The sailors were organized into companies of 200 each: the capacity at the school was 800 sailors. Each company was divided into eight section units of twenty-five men each for class units. Glenn and Randall were in Section F, *(along with Merril James Kuster of Stanley, North Dakota). Glenn belonged to Company 10E with 220 other sailors who were transferred from San Diego and Farragut. The new company was part of the Second Battalion with Ensign L. R. Miller as their Battalion Commander.

The Navy classrooms were in Building A, Industrial Arts, and the Band Building. The 16-week course in Electrical Maintenance included five courses: Mathematics, Electrical Theory, Wiring Practice, Electrical Laboratory, and Elementary Shop. The students' day began at 05:15 AM; 800 sailors went through the cafeteria line in 45 minutes. All the dorms at Iowa State were taken over by the Navy. The girls in college were moved to leased fraternity houses, as there were very few males in college during the war.

Morning Exercises began promptly at 05:45 AM, and all members of the crew needed to be present on the calisthenics location promptly. The Ship's Service Department supplied the crew with goods and services, including canteen, laundry at 50 cents per week that was returned un-ironed, the barber shop, tailoring, athletic gear and, most important of all, "mail!" Mail call was always a favorite time of day for Glenn and all the sailors throughout their service to our country. News from home and his two brothers serving in the military was always a welcomed distraction.

The station bells were struck every half hour from 0600 to 2200 to teach the sailors that every twenty-four hours was divided into six spans of four hours. In regulation with the naval time system, the bells were struck in pairs on the hour.

While Glenn and Randall attended school at Ames, the Battle of the Atlantic reached a high point. Hitler had appointed Admiral Karl Donitz to be the commanding offcer of Germany's submarine fleet. According to *Wolf Packs* by the Editors of *Time-Life Books*, Donitz developed the tactic of using a group of U-boats in a broad arc across a probable convoy route to increase the chance of one of the submarines spotting a procession of enemy ships. When ships were spotted, a submarine would radio the nearby U-boats, while continuing to track the convoy. Then the German U-boats would attack from the flanks and rear, usually on the surface at night. These groups became known as "wolf packs."

From September 1939 to September 1940, German U-boats sank 440 merchant ships and 12 enemy warships. British Prime Minister Winston Churchill later wrote that the only thing that really frightened him during the war was the steadily mounting tonnage lost to "the U-boats."

The Allies debuted their first escort carrier ships, which were joined by destroyer warships as bodyguards in a new kind of flotilla known as a Support Group. These strike groups became known by the name of "Hunter-Killers."

In May 1943, Germany lost 41 U-boat submarines to the Allies, signaling a turn in the Battle of the Atlantic (*Hunt and Kill*, p.22-23). At this point, Germany withdrew their U-Boat patrol-lines from the Atlantic and focused them on Lone-Wolf Operations.

On May 12, 1943, the last Axis army force in Africa surrendered to the Allies. Glenn's hometown friend, Harold Bach, was on the first invasion of World War II in North Africa, landing on the beaches off the Mediterranean Sea coast. Although Harold's brother was in a different Army unit, they unexpectedly encountered each other as Harold's unit drove by his brother, Archie, who was digging a fox hole in a dangerous area. The visit was joyful but brief: German planes were flying overhead.

Sixteen days later, Raymond and Lillie attended their son, Duane's graduation from flight cadet school at Craig Air Force Base in Selma, Alabama. That day on May 28, 1943, he was commissioned a second lieutenant. After basic and advanced flight school, he attended a wartime training school in southern California.

Back at the Naval Training School at Ames, Iowa, Glenn penned in his journal, "*June 12, 1943- Graduated from EM School*." At graduation the sailors were awarded a certificate from Iowa State College, and one from the Bureau of Navigation of the Navy by Commander A. F. Duernberger and College Dean, Dr. R. E. Buchanan. They were rated as Electricians Mates, Third Class, and received a corresponding increase in their pay rate. Inspired by the graduation song "Anchors Aweigh," Glenn, Randall, and new friend, Richard R. DeMarco, were among the 218 sailors that graduated that day. Two days later, June 14, 26 men received transfer orders from Ames, Iowa, Electrical Training to report to San Francisco for ship assignment.

CHAPTER 11

Ship Assignment

AFTER SIX DAYS LEAVE AND THREE days travel time, during which the new petty officers made a brief stop at their homes near Regent, North Dakota, Glenn and Randall reported for duty at San Francisco on June 23, 1943. Here they received their assignment to the USS *Guadalcanal* (CVE-60), a new flattop aircraft carrier, and were sent up the coast to Washington.

Glenn arrived at Puget Sound Naval Shipyard at Bremerton, Washington, on July 7, 1943, for Pre-commissioning school, as his ship was being prepared for duty. This school was a comprehensive crash course to prepare the recruits about the duties they would perform on their ship, and the actual machines they would have to operate. The life of everyone on the ship depended on how well they all learned to perform their duties.

The United States was rapidly turning out war machines now with crews working around the clock. Patriotism was intense and people were willing to make sacrifices. Down the coastline at San Francisco, on July 24, 1943, Glenn's brother, Wayne, married his girlfriend, Florence Crean, while on leave from the Army.

Glenn's ship, the USS *Guadalcanal*, had been converted from a Maritime Commission hull built by Kaiser Shipbuilding Co., Vancouver, Washington. A flight deck was constructed on top of the hull, along with a flight control center and a bridge. As the ship slid down the building ways on rollers on June 5, 1943, her sponsor broke a bottle of champagne over her stem, and she was named *Guadalcanal*.

Wayne and Flo (Crean) Larson

The USS *Guadalcanal* was armed with one 5-inch/38 caliber DP gun on the fantail, sixteen 40-mm AA cannons in eight twin mounts on the catwalks at the four corners of the flight deck, and twenty 20-mm AA machine guns in single mounts located along the catwalks. Each 40-mm mount was served to its own Sperry gyroscopic sight and one director located in the catwalk about ten feet away.

After *Guadalcanal's* shakedown cruise and commissioning at Astoria, Oregon, on September 25, 1943, Glenn was granted a leave and returned home to Regent.

CHAPTER 12

Romance is in the Air

WHEN GLENN'S MOTHER HEARD HE WAS coming home on leave, she quickly telephoned her closest brother, Martin Schow, of Stanton, North Dakota, with the good news. His daughters, Geneva and Mildred, were eager to visit their cousin, Glenn, but neither young woman had a driver's license. So, Geneva asked her good friend, Clara Schweigert, who had a driver's license, to come along and meet Glenn. At the time, Clara was helping her father at the Stanton Courthouse, where he was the County Judge.

Martin gave them permission to use his vehicle, as well as three containers of gasoline. Because of the war, gasoline was rationed, and they would not be able to buy any during their trip, therefore they had to take enough with them. To travel, cars were also required to have a special permission sticker in one's automobile window. Clara recalled that she rode in the front seat beside Geneva, who had a driver's permit and, whenever they met another vehicle on the road, Clara would stick her foot up on the windshield to resemble a sticker in the corner. Mildred didn't mind sitting on one of the gas containers behind the front seat during their weekend adventure.

When they arrived at Larson's farmhouse, Lillie warmly greeted the girls and then called downstairs to Glenn, where he was bathing. When he emerged from the basement without a shirt, Geneva introduced him to Clara. She was immediately impressed with the handsome sailor's charming smile, twinkle in his blue eyes, and his warm greeting. His muscular body reminded her of Charles Atlas, a well-known bodybuilder of that era.

Glenn was immediately attracted to this shy girl with dark hair and eyes, and decided to break his date with a local gal that night. Instead, he volunteered to accompany his two cousins and Clara to a dance at Mott, the neighboring town. Clara and Glenn enjoyed each other's company; in fact they were enthralled with each other, and the evening passed quickly.

When Clara returned home after the weekend, she confidently told her mother she had met her future husband. Glenn returned to Washington State for naval duty, and the two began to exchange letters and pictures.

The weekend Glenn met Clara.
Lillian, Glenn, Geneva, Clara and Mildred

Shortly before Clara and the Schow girls returned to Stanton, on September 6, 1943, Mildred's future husband, Rudy Froeschle, was shot down over Germany, along with 44 other bombers. He was serving in the Army Air Force and had co-piloted a B-17 bomber on a raid over Stuttgart that day.

Rudy spent 18 months in a German Air Force prisoner-of-war camp called Luft III with 600 other prisoners. Since the imprisoned pilots and airmen were allowed musical instruments, their band played music to muffle the sound of men digging three sophisticated tunnels. The prisoners carefully carried the dirt in their pockets, where they emptied them outside in the prison yard. Not only were the prisoners planning an escape, they were able to make their own alcohol. Rudy's trombone was fashioned into an ingenious moonshine alcohol still.

On March 24, 1944, some of these men carried out the most famous prisoner escape in Europe during WWII. The 1963 movie, *The Great Escape*, was based on the book, *The Great Escape*, by Paul Brickman, a Stalag Luft III prisoner. Luckily, Rudy chose not to go through the tunnel that night. Of the 76 men that escaped, 73 were recaptured. On personal orders of Adolf Hitler, fifty of the escapees were executed by the Gestapo by firing squad. (The murders were considered war crimes, and the trial began in 1947 in Hamburg, Germany.)

In 1943, Clara's sister, Helene, lived at Coronado in the San Diego area and was married to the career Navy man, Dick Jordan. Helene suffered from renal disease and, since her husband was usually away at sea, she encouraged Clara to come to California and live with her.

That fall, Clara purchased a train ticket to San Diego, using the money she had saved working at the Courthouse and teaching at a country school the previous winter. This prairie-grown girl of 19 had never traveled beyond North Dakota and Minnesota. Now she wondered what lay ahead in her sister's large city. To pass the time during the train trip, she wrote a letter to Glenn and tucked it into her purse.

The depot at San Diego was filled with the sights and sounds of sailors and others bustling about. Clara's eyes nervously searched the crowd for Dick, her brother-in-law, who was scheduled to meet her at the station. The crowd thinned as people grabbed their suitcases and left the area. Soon she found herself standing alone outside the depot, as it closed for the night. She became frightened, and darkness was settling in. Then, seemingly out of nowhere, a woman dressed in black stood beside her, telling her she would wait with her until her ride arrived. She told Clara that she returned to the train station every evening, hoping her husband, who was missing in action, would show up. Much to Clara's relief, the woman stayed with her and visited with her until Dick finally arrived. When Clara turned to thank the lady in black, she was gone. She later wondered if perhaps the woman was an angel, sent there to keep her safe in this strange, new city.

CHAPTER 13

Aboard the USS *Guadalcanal*

Glenn's return from North Dakota to Astoria, Oregon, was scenic as the train chugged across plains and over mountains: finally the Columbia River came into view. Astoria was primarily a salmon fishing and logging community with deep water where the Columbia River entered the ocean. It was here where Kaiser built 50 Casablanca-class Escort Carriers for the Navy, including the USS *Guadalcanal*.

On commissioning day, September 25, 1943, Glenn and Randall, along with more than 900 other sailors boarded the ship and were assigned a locker and a four-high bunk in the crew compartments.

Daniel Gallery, the ship's captain, was a confident man and set a hard pace for his crew. As they reported for duty, they received the following memo from him:

> *1. The motto of this ship will be "Can Do," meaning that we will take any tough job that is given to us and run away with it. The tougher the job, the better we will like it.*

> *2. Before a carrier can do its big job of sinking enemy ships, several hundred small jobs have got to be done and done well. One man falling down on a small job can bitch the works for the whole ship. So learn all you can about your job during this pre-commissioning period. Pretty soon we will be out where it rains bombs and it will be too late to learn.*

> *3. Note: This ship will be employed on hazardous duty. We will either sink the enemy or get sunk ourselves depending on how well we learn our*

*jobs and do our jobs later. ANYONE WHO PREFERS SAFER DUTY
SEE ME AND I WILL ARRANGE TO HAVE HIM TRANSFERRED.*

D.V. Gallery, Captain, U.S.N.

The crew wore their dress blue uniforms as they lined up on the flight deck for the commissioning ceremony. The ship's chaplain, Father Weldon, said a prayer, Captain Gallery read the orders, and they hoisted the colors. Gallery made a short speech reminding the crew that they were now the custodians of *Guadalcanal*, a name that was enshrined forever in American history. He said they would have to do great things to live up to what the Marines had already done at the island of Guadalcanal during the war in the Pacific.

The next day, after conferring with Captain Gallery and receiving his hearty approval, Father Weldon started the tradition of daily morning prayer on the ship. At 8 AM, right after colors, it was announced: "Attention to morning prayer." All hands would stop whatever they were doing, remove their caps and face the bridge for a few moments while Father Weldon shared a prayer, to which everyone joined in with, "Amen." They knew they needed God's help each day. It has been said that there are no atheists in wartime combat zones. The general morning prayer asking for God's help was welcomed and accepted by everyone.

After the ship was loaded with aircraft and refueled, it headed south to Alameda Air Station at San Francisco, cruised under the Golden Gate Bridge and passed Alcatraz Island. On October 21, 1943, Glenn wrote in his journal *"Sailed into San Francisco."*

The Guadalcanal could carry twenty-seven aircraft, and their next stop was San Diego. At this time, Glenn's brother, Duane, was training at Rice Army Air Base in the Mojave Desert of Southern California. He wrote to his uncle, Martin Schow:

> *"We got back here to Rice from maneuvers last Friday, and they gave us a few days off. I was all set to leave for Los Angeles when I got a letter from Glenn saying he was going to be in San Diego over the weekend, so I went down there. I met him uptown Saturday evening, and he stayed with me*

at the hotel as he didn't have to be back until 9:00 the next morning. He told me they were going to move the Carrier over to (Naval Air Station) North Island (at the North end of the Coronado Peninsula) the next morning. The next day about noon I took the ferry over to North Island, and just as I got there, Glenn's carrier came steaming up the bay. They docked around on the side of the island, so I took a bus over there.

While I was watching them dock it, and taxi the airplanes up that they were going to load on it, one of the pilots came over and started talking to me, and he asked me if I wanted to go aboard and look it over. Of course I did, so he took me on and had Glenn take me all over it. It is quite a contraption. Glenn has got a pretty good job on there, and the living conditions aren't bad at all. He seems to go wherever he wants to on the whole ship."

Duane continued to tell Martin that he also drove to Los Angeles and spent a night with his grandmother, Minnie, and her sister, Aunt Carrie Noben (who served as a WWI nurse in France).

Back at Coronado Island, five Eastern FM-1 *Wildcat* airplanes were loaded onboard the *Guadalcanal*, along with five Grumman TBF-1 *Avengers*, 31 officers and 47 enlisted men from Composite Squadron (VC) 36 in California.

The Grumman *Wildcats* fighter aircraft were highly maneuverable and had an aircrew of one pilot. The *Avengers* were the heaviest single-engine plane used in WWII, and they carried four depth charges weighing 500 pounds. They had limited maneuverability and the pilots said they handled like driving a truck. The *Avengers* had a three-man crew: a pilot, a radio-man/bombardier, and a rear turret gunner. Both the *Avenger* and the *Wildcat* had Grumman's patented wing design, which allowed the wings to be folded to use less storage space on the hangar deck. Both were equipped with the new ASV Mark III radar.

An eight-day cruise in southern California waters allowed the transferred pilots to break into their new jobs and gave them a chance to complete their qualifications. They also completed training in night flying.

Landing on a flight deck is one of the most difficult things a navy pilot will ever do. Heavy steel arresting cables or wires stretch across the ship's flight deck to catch an aircraft's tail hook and bring the plane to a stop. *Guadalcanal's* flight deck was 477-feet long and 80-feet wide, half the length of the flight deck of a fleet carrier. There were two elevators on the deck, one forward and one aft. The arresting gear consisted of nine wires and three barriers. Each hydraulic arresting unit controlled two wires and were located in pairs at the back of the ship directly beneath the flight deck.

Morning dawned very still on the day the pilots were scheduled for their first landing on the *Guadalcanal*. A headwind was usually helpful, but Capt. Gallery was undaunted as he made the ship's first take-off and landing while flying a North American SNJ-4 *Texan*. Landing on an escort carrier required extraordinary skill and courage and the flight deck crew erupted into loud cheers.

In his book, *My Navy Career,* Howard Sherer recalled, "*Captain Gallery took off in a SNJ Trainer, made a turn at port, entered the landing pattern and made a beautiful landing. We were now a real official carrier. This was a rare happening, as not too many captains made the first landing on their carriers we were told.*"

The pilots experienced their first catapult launches, and the unit began to get the feel of duty afloat. A single compressed-air powered hydraulic catapult was located on the port side of the flight deck. Sherer wrote:

> "*Flight operations are always a dramatic event. When I was on gun watch you could almost reach out and touch the planes as they took off, drop down a little and then start her climb. When they were catapulted off this was really dramatic. The catapult captain would give the pilot the sign to rev her (engine) up to full power, when ready the pilot would give his thumbs up signal, then the catapult director would give the signal to launch and the plane would be literally shot off the flight deck" (p.7). If a pilot would overshoot the landing area on the deck, he would have to abort the landing and climb quickly or he could end up in the sea.*"

After they finished their qualifications on the second day, the five *Avengers* flew 11 pilots to San Diego NAS to bring back the planes they had left at North Island. The ship also carried out gunnery practice, fire drill, life raft drills, and instructions on seamanship, swimming, airplane and ship identification, and physical fitness training.

On November 15, *Guadalcanal*, accompanied by the escort carrier, USS *Mission Bay (CVE 59)* and destroyer USS *Welles (DD-628)* sailed south, working their way to the Atlantic through the Panama Canal. Capt. Gallery wrote, *"All those Kaiser ships started off with the greenest and most inexperienced crews that ever put to sea. The average age of our lads was about twenty-one, and over eighty percent of them had never seen salt water before" (Clear the Decks*, Daniel V. Gallery, 1951, p. 58).

Early on Thanksgiving morning, the *Guadalcanal* tied up at Balboa port in central Panama, and the crew was served a delicious holiday meal. The liberty party went ashore after lunch, but the men found Balboa lacked entertainment and scenery, so the ship moved on to Panama City.

Here, some of the sailors thought the narrow streets and projecting second- story balconies with lattice railings looked like the old French Quarter of New Orleans, Louisiana. A great stench from the slums became annoying in the humid air, and it rained intermittently. The next day, *Guadalcanal* passed through the Panama Canal and was damaged entering a lock when one of her 40-millimeter gun tubs was fouled. They stopped for three days at Colon to repair the gun and surrounding hull, then continued on their way.

The German submarine, *U-516*, was reported to be sinking ships in the nearby Caribbean waters, so *Guadalcanal* and *Mission Bay* were directed to search for the U-boat. All of the available *Avengers* flew a five and a half-hour search, but were unsuccessful in locating the sub. Meanwhile, in December 1943, Germany's *U-505* departed Lorient, France, with her new captain, Harold Lange.

Lorient was the most heavily bombed French Atlantic U-boat base that year and, by December, it was mostly a ghost city. (*Hunt&Kill*, p.86-88.) By operating from the French ports, U-boats transit time was reduced. The proximity allowed them to reach the ocean faster, and gave them as much as a week longer to hunt the enemy before returning to the French ports. As previously mentioned, they had broken the British naval codes and were well informed about the makeup and movement of Allied convoys.

Around this same time, the Allies developed a new system called Huff-Duff that could clearly register surfaced U-boats up to a 12-miles radius.

Germany's Donitz noticed the Allies' apparent ability to locate the wolf packs at great distances, and the radar they were aware of could not explain this. Repeated rerouting of Allied convoys indicated special knowledge, and Donitz suspected treason. It was Britain's sophisticated ship-and-shore based high-frequency direction-finding equipment, Huff-Duff, which picked up U-boat radio traffic, which allowed the position of a transmission to be fixed by triangulation. Dönitz now abandoned the group tactics and deployed U-boats as "lone wolves" on lonely, dangerous patrols.

Guadalcanal and its group sailed into Norfolk, Virginia, on December 3. Glenn and his fellow sailors beheld a feverishly busy seaport with ships of all sizes tied up to the piers. Huge cranes groaned, and men shouted as ships were loaded and unloaded. Small tractors hastily pulled trailers with supplies and, nearby seagulls cawed and fluttered over the ocean as they attempted to feed on fish.

The city was not terribly friendly, and a sea of white Navy caps filled the bustling downtown area and entertainment centers. Christmas came and, for some of the homesick sailors, this was their first time away from home for the holiday.

This was actually Glenn's second Christmas away from home, as he had spent his first one in boot camp at Farragut, Idaho. Although homesick, his good friend, Randall, was with him to share stories and memories of their hometown, Regent. That same year, in 1943, Bing Crosby recorded the song "I'll be Home for Christmas, If only in my dreams," which became a top 10 hit. Tears formed in Clara's eyes and trickled down her cheeks as she listened to the same melancholic song on the radio, along with thousands of other Americans back home.

While at Norfolk, Glenn took the rating examination and was promoted to Electrician Mate 2nd Class on New Year's Day. Four days later, the *Guadalcanal* became the flagship of the newly formed Anti-submarine Task Group 21.12, along with four escort destroyers (ED) to protect her.

Glenn and crew excitedly wondered what lie ahead as their first mission at sea began.

CHAPTER 14

First Anti-Submarine Warfare Cruise

Glenn's journal: *"January 20, 1944,- Sailed into Casablanca, North Africa.*
Sank two German U-Boats."

AFTER REPAIRS AND ALTERATIONS, SUPPLIES WERE loaded at Norfolk and preparations for departure were completed. Task Group 21.12, *Guadalcanal* and her four escort destroyer ships, the DDs *Alden, John D. Edwards, Whipple and John D. Ford,* departed Hampton Roads, Norfolk, on January 5, 1944, bound for the Cape Verde Islands, off the coast of Africa.

Since the destroyer was the only surface ship that could effectively locate, attack and destroy a submarine, smaller versions were built for fleet assignment during WWII. They had a tighter turning radius and more specialized armament than fleet destroyers.

Destroyer Escort (DE) was the US Navy classification for these ships that were first built to escort and protect the ocean merchant convoys. Soon they played a significant role in combination with escort aircraft carriers (CVE) to form Hunter-Killer task groups in the Battle of the Atlantic. The DE was much more maneuverable than destroyers and had the latest equipment in antisubmarine warfare (ASW), which included sonar echo with an underwater detection range of two miles. Supersonic sound travels in a straight line and if it strikes a solid, metal object, it bounces back and is detected by instruments as audible "pings." The DEs also had surface search radar and air search radar.

The *Guadalcanal* Task Group's mission was to search for enemy submarines in the North Atlantic Ocean, along the United States to Gibraltar convoy route. Gibraltar is a narrow peninsula three miles long on Spain's southern Mediterranean coast. It is a heavily fortified British air and naval base that guards the Strait of Gibraltar, which is the only entrance to the Mediterranean Sea from the Atlantic Ocean.

Lt. Commander Adrian H. Perry, veteran VC-13 squadron commander, was on board *Guadalcanal* with twenty-one aircraft; 9 *FM-1 Wildcats* and 12 *FBF-1c Avengers*. By 8 PM the first evening at sea, the weather had turned very stormy, and tragically, a lookout sailor was washed overboard. Despite a search operation the man was never found in the turbulent sea. Two *Wildcats* were badly damaged that night during flight operations and were offloaded in Bermuda three days later.

The stormy weather continued, and on January 10, 1944, an *Avenger*, manned by Lt. James F. Schoby, ARM 1c Almon R. Martin, and AMM2 James A. Lavender, launched for a patrol. Their weight was 16,700 pounds, which included six rockets under the wings, two 360-pound depth charges in the bomb bay, machine gun ammunition, and fuel. The stormy weather and heavy waves pounded *Guadalcanal*, so Capt. Gallery recalled the planes.

The *Avenger* received two wave-offs and, on the third attempt to land, the plane rolled over on its back, the nose fell, and it crashed over the side of the carrier. It entered the ocean upside down about 50 feet from the ship and sank in barely 40 seconds. Lavender swam to the surface and was picked up by a destroyer. Five minutes after the *Avenger* sank, a depth charge exploded at about 250 feet. The destroyer searched for about an hour after picking up Lavender, but Schoby and Martin were not found and perished in the cold waters. Earlier, Schoby had received the Distinguished Flying Cross for his part in sinking *U-487* on July 13, 1943, from the escort carrier USS *Core*.

Heavy seas continued and, two hours later, another *Avenger* landed in the catwalk and had to be jettisoned to clear the flight deck for the plane in the air that was running low on fuel. All of the crewmen of the last two aircraft to land survived.

Six days later, January 16, two *Avenger* aircraft flown by Ensigns Bert Hudson and William McLane from *Guadalcanal* sighted submarines refueling on the surface of the ocean several hundred miles west of the Azores. During this period, U-boats seldom surfaced during daylight hours. It was an overcast day and about 20 minutes before sunset when two *Avengers* on their return to the ship spotted three surfaced U-Boats. In a refueling operation, the larger "milk cow tanker sub" *U-544*, was supplying oil to *U-516*, with the other U-boat (*U-129*) waiting its turn. A re-fueler submarine was equipped with extra fuel tanks and was responsible for re-supplying attack U-boats, to allow them to remain on patrol longer.

U-129 dived and disappeared. The planes plastered depth charges and rockets around the two U-boats, but because they were connected with mooring lines and fuel hoses, they were unable to submerge quickly. U-544 went down slowly by the stern, with her bow high in the air, as men jumped overboard. Debris and German sailors were seen in a large pool of oil. All three subs disappeared and cheers went up all over the ship when the loudspeakers announced that they had blasted two subs to the bottom. It was their first kill, and now they were seasoned combat members of the Atlantic Fleet team. Actually, U-516 was only damaged and was able to regain control and move out of the area. Two destroyers were sent to pick-up survivors but none was found.

Guadalcanal had eight planes in the air, and now Capt. Gallery recalled them, as darkness set in. He wrote:

"But curiosity is a strong human emotion. This was a first kill and that oil puddle with the Germans paddling around in it was only 40 miles from the ship. I had detached a destroyer to pick up survivors, but every one of our pilots felt it was essential to the war effort for him to fly over there and take a gander at the scene. We put out some preemptory orders on the rail to 'get the hell back here and land'. But the boys later claimed there was a lot of static.

At this stage of the war, we were all still primarily day-time pilots in the jeep carriers. Even on the big carriers in the Pacific, night flying was regarded as a hazardous business to be undertaken by a few highly trained specialists. Landing on a jeep (small carrier) after dark was perhaps three or four times as difficult as landing on a big carrier, because of the tiny deck, greater motion of the ship, and slower speed. By the time my pilots came wandering back from their rubberneck trip, the sun had gone down, and under that solid overcast, darkness was rapidly closing in on us.

The first four lads got aboard o.k., but the fifth one landed too far
to starboard and wound up with his right wheel down in the galley
walkway and his left wing and tail sticking out over the deck, fouling
the landing area. We still had three planes in the air, and the darkness
was getting blacker every minute." (Twenty Million Tons Under the Sea,
Daniel V. Gallery, 1956, 2018, p. 202).

The fouled flight deck was cleared by crewmen by cutting off the tail of the damaged plane, but the sun set, and the two remaining Avengers, including Hudson's, were running short of fuel. Some of the aviators believed a third submarine was in the area, but Capt. Gallery grew increasingly worried about the chances of the pilots' survival and ordered *Guadalcanal* to turn on her lights. He later explained "*In this case, we had no choice. To have any chance of getting our boys aboard, we had to turn on the lights.*" Gallery told the pilots, "*That tail doesn't stick out very far into the landing area. If you land smack on the center line, your right wing will clear it. So just ignore that plane on the starboard side...come in and land.*" *Twenty Million Tons Under the Sea*, Daniel Gallery, p. 203).

The rapidly deteriorating conditions made the pilots nervous, and Hudson landed but went through the barriers and over the port side of the ship into the sea upside down. A destroyer fished all three men out of the water unhurt. After that, Gallery ordered all the ships to turn on their search lights, and the last two pilots to ditch (into the ocean) alongside the destroyers. They were fished out of the water, the lights were turned out, and the Task Group "got the hell out of that area."

Casablanca, Morocco, South Africa, hosted the Casablanca Conference in 1943, in which Churchill and Roosevelt discussed the progress of the war. The Allies gave top priority to defeating the U-boats at the conference. Subsequent bombing of the bases on the Bay of Biscay, France, had little effect on the 23-feet thick concrete submarine bunkers built by Hitler to house his submarines.

Casablanca was a strategic port and had been taken by the Allies in Operation Torch in 1942. It was the site of a large American air base, which was the staging area for all American aircraft in the European Theater of Operations during WWII.

At Casablanca, the sailors were warned to not flirt with the women, as the natives' Islam religion strictly forbade it. While *Guadalcanal* was moored, some of the men on shore leave, including Glenn, traveled to Rabat, the capital city. That day the sailors were entertained watching the colorful pageantry of a military parade as it passed in review of Sultan Mohammad V of Morocco. It was a hot day and Glenn and the other sailors were offered a drink of water from a goat-skin bag. Historically, some Moroccan men had a job of walking around and selling water from a goat-skin bag. They would wear a necklace of metal cups that they used to distribute the water. Obviously, sharing the same cup was not a very sanitary practice. Little did they know that this small act would possibly have future consequences.

After replenishment at Casablanca, the *Guadalcanal* Task Group left port for Norfolk on January 29th. They had lost two pilots, three air crewmen, and six *Avenger* planes.

Capt. Gallery spent the remainder of the cruise relentlessly drilling the crash crew about clearing a fouled deck. He timed the crew and had them roll the damaged *Avenger* over to the edge of the deck, ease one wheel into the cat walk, and then wrestle it back up on the flight deck. After daily practice, they were able to remove any wreck in under four minutes. They also searched for U-boats on their return voyage and found none. They anchored at Bermuda for seven hours and unloaded two *Wildcat* planes that sustained severe damage. The carrier's escorts were then detached for duties elsewhere.

Upon return to Norfolk, Glenn was granted a five-day leave of absence from February 17 to February 22, 1944. During this time, his good friend, Randall Novak, was transferred to the USS *Bennington*, a huge aircraft carrier, which left New York and transited the Panama Canal. This carrier participated in the Pacific war against Japan, and her planes assisted in the sinking of the Japanese battleship *Yamato*.

Back at Norfolk, Capt. Gallery proposed the idea of round-the-clock flight operations as soon as they experienced a "good moon and a reasonable sea." A full moon would enable the crew to see to take off and land. And Gallery surmised that, as the moon went through its phases, the men would adjust. Although the *Avengers* were equipped with radar, the crews usually needed to see their targets, as well.

Duane Schow Larson flew 68 combat missions in a P-51 Mustang

While Glenn was on leave, his brother, Duane, who had advanced flight training at Rice Army Air Force base in southern California's Mojave Desert's Rice Valley, was assigned to the 8th Air Force at Fowlmere, England. Fowlmere Airfield was known as "the Hen Puddle" due to the wet conditions during the winter of 1943-1944.

During WWII the 8th Air Force formed the greatest air armada in history, and is commonly known as the 'Mighty Eighth." In late February, Allied air forces in Europe bombed Germany's aircraft industries with overwhelming force for five days. The commanding general of the U.S. Army Air Force reported "those five days changed the history of the air war."

Duane and the 504th Fighter Squadron, under the 339th Fighter Group, flew their new P-51 *Mustangs* in operations starting the end of April 1944. In the space of one year, the 339th had the highest claims of air and ground enemy aircraft victories. On May 22, 1944, Duane was promoted to 1st Lieutenant with the 8th AF.

Germany's Commander-in-Chief of the Luftwaffe had boasted that Allied bombers would never reach Berlin, but they did. Beginning as early as August 1940, and Germany's capital became the most bombed-out city in Europe.

Duane eventually completed 68 missions with his *Mustang* P-51 single-seat fighter aircraft. He escorted B-17 bombers all over France and Germany, including Berlin, providing protection against German fighters.

While Duane was flying his single-seat fighter in Europe, Robert Nasset, a New England, North Dakota, native was flying a C-46 cargo plane over the Hump on the eastern end of the Himalayan Mountains. He had enlisted in the Army Air Corps in 1942 and trained as a pilot.

After Japan cut off the last land route to China, the Burma Road, supplies could not be delivered to Chinese forces fighting Japan. The United States began the Army Air Forces' most dangerous airlift route. Aid had to come by air and American planes had to come from the West, over the "Roof of the World."

"Flying the Hump" over the Himalayan Mountains was vitally important to winning the war, and incredibly dangerous. More than 1,000 men and 600 planes were lost over the 530-mile stretch of rugged, frozen terrain. In fact, the extreme weather took down more US pilots than the Japanese. Robert Nasset was one of the heroic Flying the Hump pilots that delivered around 650,000 tons of material to China at great cost of lives during the missions' 42-month history. Robert lost many of his buddies in the war, never flew again, married Shirley Prince, and raised his family on a farm northeast of Regent after the war.

Glenn's high school classmate, Doyle Gordon, entered the Army in 1943 and served as a radio operator in the China Burma and India Theatre. Using the Morris Code, he communicated with the bombers and other aircraft.

Another pilot that Flew the Hump was Duane Larson's friend, Ell Torrance, of Bismarck, North Dakota. After the war, Ell and Duane showcased their flying skills at many barn storming air shows around the state. First Lieutenant Torrance also served in Korea from January 1951 to September 1952.

CHAPTER 15

Second Antisubmarine Warfare Cruise

Glenn's photo - TBM in front on Guadalcanal, Note the Wildcat with wings folded, back left

AFTER NINE FM-2 *WILDCATS*, THREE TBF-1Cs, and nine Eastern TBM-1C *Avengers* were loaded, *Guadalcanal's* Task Group eased out of the port at Norfolk, Virginia, on March 7, 1944, bound for Casablanca, Morocco, on their second ASW cruise.

The Battle of the Atlantic continued, as Germany's U-boat crews destroyed forty-one Allied ships in the first ten days of March and sank more than 100,000 tons that month. Karl Donitz, Germany's Supreme Commander of the Navy, realized that surface warfare for U-boats had come to an end due to better radar detection by the Allies. They now operated mostly underwater but needed to surface on a regular basis to recharge their batteries.

Five escort destroyers screened the carrier as they hunted for U-boats. The weather was often overcast, clouds frequently blocked the moonlight, and the rough seas pounded the ship. Capt. Gallery launched aircraft from dawn to dusk in areas where analysts believed that enemy submarines lurked, but with no success. On March 22, planes dropped sonobuoys (small sonar system buoys with radio transmitters) when they detected an apparent U-boat, but she got away.

The task group arrived at Casablanca on March 27, and everyone was able to go ashore for liberty. Some of the shore party enjoyed a French military parade and a beer party. After refueling, the convoy left Casablanca on March 30. The Tenth Fleet Headquarters sent a high priority message that a submarine (*U-515*) was operating about 200 miles from their location.

Coming out of the Bay of Biscay off the western coast of France in early April, *U-505* silently passed by the USS *Guadalcanal* and her task group undetected. However, they were bound by fate to meet again later.

For entertainment the *Guadalcanal* held boxing matches in an improvised ring and musical shows in the hangar deck. A skit was performed in which crewmen captured Adolf Hitler, who was played by the ship's doctor.

Two U-boats

On a clear, dark night at sea, the whole world can be filled with brilliant stars, like diamonds sparkling against a black velvet dome. Perhaps looking out into the universe, Glenn was sometimes reminded of one of his mother's favorite Bible verses from Psalm 8: 3-5: "When I consider your heavens, the work of your fingers, the moon and the stars which you have set in place, what is mankind that you are mindful of them, human beings that you care for them? You have made them a little lower than the angels and crowned them with glory and honor."

That calm night, April 9, 1944, a full moon reflected off the sea, and *Guadalcanal* sent up four heavily armed *Avengers* to search the area. One of the pilots saw a U-boat on the ocean surface recharging its batteries, but the radio report failed, and he returned to the ship.

Capt. Gallery launched two more *Avengers* to fly over the area. Twenty-seven minutes after midnight Germany's Captain Werner Henke's submarine, *U-515*, was discovered by radar and then sighted. An *Avenger* aircraft flew behind the moonlight's refection on the water and dropped depth charges across the submarine.

Henke was a Nazi war hero and holder of the Knight's Cross with Oak Leaves, one of the aces of the U-boat fleet. He had 150,000 tons of Allied shipping sunk, to his credit. He temporarily escaped as the aircraft circled, but a destroyer tracked the deeply submerged U-boat by sound indication. Ten planes made several coordinated attacks on the sub with rockets and depth charges throughout the night.

The *U-515*'s log revealed that all within the sub were aware that it was Henke's intention to torpedo the *Guadalcanal* if at all possible. When he heard the ship's sonar pinging on him, though, he immediately took evasive action.

The *Pope* destroyer maintained contact with *U-515* all morning, fired hedgehogs and depth charges, then lost contact. *U-515* attempted to escape, did evasive maneuvers, went deep, released decoys, and even released oil and debris, but her air supply was nearly exhausted, and her batteries were low on charge.

Chatelain regained contact and fired 13 depth-charges in sequence. Julian Austin, age 96, of Marion, North Carolina, was a Torpedo Mate 2C on the starboard quarter of the rear end of *Chatelain*. He recalled,

> "My battle station was as phone talker and captain of the starboard K- Guns. These were located on the rear of the ship.... The first charges dropped had begun to explode when suddenly, about 75 yards off our starboard beam, the U-515 shot out of the water bow first with water streaming off her deck. One of our depth charges from the starboard K-guns landed on the deck of the sub and rolled off."

German sailors rushed out of the conning tower and jumped into the sea. Austin continued,

> "Then all hell broke loose. Here we were eyeball to eyeball with a wounded U-boat within shouting distance.... This was the first enemy surface target we had ever faced and everyone was a little nervous.... Every gun on our starboard side began firing and getting good hits. We could even

*hear the explosion of the shells hitting the sub. One man seemed to be
heading for the deck gun to return fire when he was hit by a 20mm shell,
and blown overboard. All the men in the water began swimming toward
the* Chatelain. *An Avenger from the carrier roared overhead, firing her
guns and rockets into the sub." (Julian Austin, July 7, 2020 interview and
report). The U.S.S. Flaherty* also fired at the submarine.

Subsequent damage caused water and oil to enter the U-boat, and Henke
was forced to surface at 3 p.m. right in the middle of the waiting ships.
U-515 had been in a perfect position to sink one or more of the destroyers by
torpedoes or gunfire but was immediately devastated by point-blank gunfire
and rockets. As *Wildcat* fighters from *Guadalcanal* strafed (attacked repeatedly
with machine-gun fire) the sub and her captain, Werner Henke, U-boot ace,
opened the conning tower hatch. When he saw three destroyers, he ordered
his crew to abandon the ship. They scrambled on deck and jumped overboard
as fast as possible.

The sub upended and sank within five minutes. Sixteen crew members
died from the combined fire of the destroyers and airplanes. Forty-four
survivors, including Captain Henke, were taken aboard the destroyers.
However, they were later transferred to the *Guadalcanal* by breeches buoy, a
crude device similar to a zip line, used to transfer people from ship to ship
by means of a rope and pulley between them. Whenever prisoners or rescued
downed pilots were transferred this way, *Guadalcanal* sent a container of ice
cream back to the destroyer via the breeches buoy.

Captain Gallery wrote:

> *"The prisoners were well behaved and very cooperative. They were very
> glad to be coming to the United States. Each was given a cot and a
> mattress, and they were served the same food as the ship's crew. One
> toilet and washroom were set aside for their exclusive use. We gave them
> daily exercises in small groups."*

Henke understood English and had worked in the Boston and Philadelphia
shipyards before the war. He had his first naval experience on board German

battleships. After serving on U-124, he became Captain of U-515 in February 1942. He sank 24 merchant ships and two warships before he was captured and imprisoned at Fort Hunt, Virginia. He greatly feared he would be turned over to the British and tried as a war criminal. June 15, 1944, it was reported that Henke walked to the prison yard fence in broad daylight and slowly began to climb it.

Guards shouted for him to stop, but he continue to climb and was fatally shot. It was thought most likely to be a suicide attempt. (uboat.net, Top U-boat Aces, The Men, Werner Henke).

U-68

The next day was Easter Sunday, April 10, 1944. At 2 AM, with the flight deck badly pitching in the waves, an *Avenger* crashed into the barrier as it landed. There was slight damage to the propeller. Two hours later, pilot Lt. S.G. Parsons, flying his *Avenger* #24 on instruments, followed radar indication and broke into a clear spot. He sighted a U-boat and made two attacks. The sub submerged in extremely poor visibility, and a glow was observed under the water.

Around 6:30 AM, Lt. Parsons' plane again broke through a clear spot in the clouds and sighted a fully surfaced submarine. The lookout on *U-68* reported the approach of enemy aircraft and took his station at his 37-millimeter gun. He delivered 200 rounds of heavy anti-aircraft fire. While one *Avenger* strafed from astern, two other planes delivered four attacks.

Suddenly, the U-boat siren sounded for an emergency crash dive. The lookout, 19-year-old Seaman 2nd Class, Hans Kastrup, helped secure the 37-mm gun and noticed that one of the gunners had been wounded. He struggled forward with the wounded man, attempting to bring him into the sub. As they approached the conning tower hatch, it slammed shut, and the U-boat began to submerge. The two men were left behind, and Kastrup must have thought this was the worst day of his life.

In the water, they were pulled under by the sinking submarine's suction, but surfaced clear of the boat. There was a terrific underwater explosion followed by large air bubbles, oil, debris, battery acid, and torpedo air flasks floating up. Again, there was a large glowing light underwater.

Kastrup's lifejacket was punctured by bullets, but for some time, he continued to hold onto the man wounded in the stomach and leg. The injured man turned very pale, became unconscious, and did not survive. Finally, one of the planes dropped a rubber boat, and after some time passed, USS *Chatelain* came alongside and transferred Hans Kastrup to *Guadalcanal*.

Chances of survival for U-boat crew men were becoming increasingly small. Perhaps it wasn't the young lad's worst day ever after all. Following the war, Hans Kastrup remembered that the Americans stood by to rescue any survivors, and he sent Capt. Gallery an annual Easter card.

Glenn's souvenir paperweight

Three torpedo submarine air flasks were picked up at the scene of the sinking, and later Guadalcanal machinists cut the heavy steel to make 2 x 4 inch engraved paper weights. Glenn proudly brought one of these souvenirs home with him after the war.

U-68 was one of the most successful U-boats, conducting ten patrols, and sinking thirty-two merchant ships and one auxiliary warship. *U-68* sank northwest of the Portuguese Island of Madeira, along with Commander Lauzemis and fifty-five of his men.

As Captain Gallery reflected on the U-515 and U-68 events, he began to wonder if they could have captured a U-boat instead of sinking it. He began formulating a plan and directed each ship in the task group to prepare and train a boarding party to seize, board, and tow an enemy submarine if the opportunity arose.

The task group refueled at Fayal in the Azores and arrived home safely on April 26, 1944, ending the Second ASW Cruise. Guadalcanal detached the escort destroyers, unloaded the squadron at Norfolk and left the ship at the Norfolk Navy Yard for repairs. Glenn wrote, "*Returned to Navy Yard at Portsmouth on April 30,1944,*" and the crew was given two weeks' liberty.

During this time, Gallery marched over to Washington, D.C., where he visited the Tenth Fleet's F-21, the U-boat tracking room. There he spoke to Commander Kenneth A. Knowles, who headed the Atlantic Section, Combat Intelligence Division, of the Headquarters of the Commander-in-Chief, United States Fleet. Knowles had expanded and developed the initial anti-submarine section and later organized and led the division. He evaluated the enemy situation in the Atlantic and gave direct support of the Allied operations.

Prior to the cruise departure, the Hunter-Killer task group held a conference in Norfolk with the ships' skippers and several experts from the Washington staff. After the usual discussion on communication and search plans for air and surface operations, Capt. Gallery told the group of his plan to try to capture a seaworthy U-boat after bringing it to the surface. He figured that if they would blast the submarine briskly with small-caliber guns they could force the German's overboard, and boarding parties could attempt to keep her afloat.

He wrote,

"*I want each ship to organize a boarding party and have a whale boat (provisioned with the materials and equipment) ready to lower throughout the next cruise. Also, keep your tow line where you can get at it in case we need it. Any questions?*"

He envisioned the boarding parties would disarm the demolition charges and close all valves to prevent scuttling (sinking of a ship by allowing water to flow into the hull) so that they could recover all the intelligence materials on the U-boat.

Silence followed, and the meeting was adjourned.

CHAPTER 16

Third Anti-Submarine Warfare Cruise and U-505 Cruise to Cape Verde Islands

GUADALCANAL AND HER DESTROYER ESCORTS, CHATELAIN, *Flaherty, Jenks, Pillsbury and Pope,* (Task Group 22.3) departed from Hampton Roads on May 15, 1944. As they cleared the Virginia Capes the next day, Capt. Gallery signaled each ship to organize their boarding party and keep a whale boat ready to lower in a hurry. He related, *"I think most of the boys who were named for the boarding parties figured, 'What the hell, this will never come off, I might as well get credit for volunteering.' But whatever their reasons, we got plenty of volunteers."* And Glenn was one of them.

Codebreakers at Bletchley Park in Britain, with the help of American allies, broke the German Enigma cipher, and the U.S. Navy knew the approximate location of a U-boat off the coast of West Africa. Through prisoners' of war interrogations, drawings of the interiors of various types of U-boats were made and shared with the boarding parties.

Gallery now plunged into full-scale, round the clock flying. All the pilots of the new squadron were checked out for night take-offs and landings, and they started during a full moon. The operation continued as the moon waned, and soon they were landing in pitch dark. Gallery said it was possible to do this because of the splendid basic training the pilots got at Pensacola.

Unfortunately, one morning the pilot of an Avenger forgot to shift his gas valve from the port to the starboard tank, causing him to run out of gas and his engine quit. He flipped his valve to the starboard tank and, in 30 seconds the engine started again, and he resumed his flight to the ship. He reported this incident by radio to the ship, but he had two inexperienced crewmen who were filling in during this routine training mission. One radio man in the plane panicked and yelled, *"Bail out,"* which he did. The other man bailed, also, but either didn't pull his rip cord or was too low for his chute to open. The first man came down in the water safely and inflated his Mae West life jacket. The other man plummeted down into the water and didn't come up again.

The pilot landed unaware of this incident, and the flight deck crew found the escape hatch open and the occupants missing. The sea was calm, which allowed search planes to locate a green dye marker in the water. A few hours later, an escort destroyer reached the spot and recovered one man.

During Capt. Gallery's training, there were many crash landings. When the night landing qualifications ended, one-third of their aircraft were damaged or deadlined (unable to fly), but there were no fatalities.

For three weeks, up in the air they scoured around the Cape Verde Islands with four airplanes around the clock. The five destroyer escorts faced out 3,000 yards ahead of *Guadalcanal*, providing a screen for her. But no submarines were sighted, and things were getting quite dull. Capt. Gallery recalled that sub hunting is a tedious, dull job 99 percent of the time. Airplanes could only spot U-boats when they were surfaced, but now they were submerged most of the time. The destroyers' sonar range was about 2,000 yards, and the U-boats could hear ships an hour away. A submarine had two options, go deeper or burst ahead and run on the surface, but both used valuable battery power.

To break the monotony of the days, an updated list of "The Boarding Party" was posted daily, with periodical drills. Gallery and his officers revised the original boarding party almost daily for three weeks to get the best-qualified people. Glenn would check the list on the Bulletin Board, and when the signal "Away Boarders" was announced, he said that he and the other boarders rushed into their whale boat, lowered it into the sea, and maneuvered it in a circle around the *Guadalcanal*.

When not on duty, Glenn was busy writing return letters to Clara. The romance grew, and in one letter, he proposed marriage to her. She quickly wrote back, "*Yes.*" It was both an exciting and stressful time, as they did not know when or if they would see each other again as the World War pressed on.

Meanwhile, on May 29, communicators decoded a top-secret message from a task group several hundred miles from them. It announced that their sister ship, the *Block Island*, a submarine hunter aircraft carrier, had just been torpedoed and sunk off the Canary Islands. *U-549* had slipped undetected through her destroyer escorts' screen. Capt. Gallery called an assembly on the flight deck the next morning and broke the sobering news to the crewmen. He then asked, *"Does this news scare us?"* After 15 seconds, he said, *"I can see the answer in your faces, and the answer is, 'Hell, no!' To tell the truth, the actual answer was, 'You're damned right, it does and that went for me, too."*

After three weeks of hunting for U-boats, the Hunter-Killer Task Group was running low on fuel and started toward Casablanca on May 30. As they worked their way north toward the Bay of Biscay, they received information from Washington's CIC that a U-Boat was homeward bound along this same route. For four days, the Task Group picked up radio transmissions from a U-Boat, and the pilots relayed that they heard submarine propeller noises from the sonar buoys they had dropped. *U-505* stayed submerged most of the time, as they could detect the Task Group's radar.

On June 2, 1944, Captain Lange decided to keep his sub on the surface longer in an attempt to recharge the batteries. *U-505* evaded discovery, but the effort failed to completely recharge the batteries, however, and she continued to operate at a disadvantage because of low electricity.

In *Steel Boat, Iron Hearts*, Hans Goebeler, an enlisted man working in *U-505*'s control room, wrote:

> *"We knew we were in a tight spot. For three days, (June 1-3), we could not surface for more than a few minutes before our radar warning gear let out its scream of alarm. The air inside the boat grew so stale we were forced to don the hated personal rebreathing devices to stay alive. Even worse, our battery charge was reaching a critically low level. We had to get out of the area."*

Captain Lange ordered the U-boat to surface and make a high-speed run back toward the African coast the afternoon of June 3. The lookouts found the sky empty of planes and clouds, and they ran 85 miles to the east. Now, *U-505*'s battery was recharged, and the ship was ventilated. Lange submerged and set a course north for Lorient, unaware they were on a collision course with an American "Hunter-Killer" task group.

On June 3, 1944, Hunter Killer Task Group 22.3 picked up transmissions on a U-Boat frequency. Late in the afternoon, Capt. Gallery convinced his chief engineer, Earl Trosino, that they probably had enough fuel to work back over the same area all night. The captain kept the *Avengers* flying patrol all night, and although they heard propeller sounds from the sonobuoys that had dropped in the water, there with no aerial sightings.

Sunday, June 4, 1944, dawned beautiful and clear with a slight breeze. The captain recovered the *Avengers* and launched two *Wildcats* for daytime patrol. Torsino approached him with his fuel report and stated, *"You better pray hard at mass this morning, Captain; you used more fuel last night than I thought you would."* With regret, Gallery reluctantly turned the Task Group north toward Casablanca.

While he ate breakfast, Gallery looked over the *Guadalcanal's* Plan of the Day sheet, which was formulated the night before. One item on it was the list of names entitled, *"Final Crew for Captured U-boat."* Gallery and his officers had been revising the original boarding party almost daily for three weeks to get the best qualified people for the party. Plenty of eager sailors who had never seen a submarine, except for the U-515, volunteered for this duty. They wanted men for the boarding party who had some knowledge they might put to use, men who knew something about diesel engines, men who knew something about storage batteries, or men who had served in a submarine. The only man who had served in a U.S. submarine became their sub "expert." He had been a yeoman (one who performs clerical work) on an S-boat and could tell them about the paperwork or filing system on a submarine. The Final Boarding Party List was posted for the ship's sailors to see, and Glenn Larson was excited to see his name was still on it.

At the morning worship service on the hangar deck, Gallery prayed for Divine intervention in getting his ship into the harbor at Casablanca. He returned to the flight deck and sat in his skipper chair on the bridge, sipping a cup of coffee. He was still fuming over the fact that a submarine had gotten away from them.

At 11:00 AM, the carrier hoisted signal flags to change course and head into the wind to land the returning planes. Julian Austin, *Chatalain* Torpedo Mate, reported that all the destroyers began making turns to assume the protective screen around the carrier. His ship, the *Chatelain*, was coming around at flank speed to maintain their position in the maneuver when the sonar man reported a strong contact on a sub.

That morning, *U-505's* Capt. Lange decided to chart a course closer to the Cape Verde Islands to shorten the return journey, and he ran the submerged submarine slowly northward. Their battery was reaching a critically low level. In *Steel Boat, Iron Hearts*, Hans Goebeler, the crewman on *U-505* wrote, "We were low on oxygen so everyone not on duty was confined to their bunks to conserve air. I laid there in that stinking bunk, whispering prayers from the little black Bible my mother had given me when I joined the Kreigmarine" (Nazi Germany Navy).

By noon, Goebeler was back on duty in the control room. As the smell of hot coffee drifted through the sub, the hydrophone sound man reported faint propeller noises coming from several distant points off the submarine's stern. Capt. Lange suspected a convoy might be passing by and ordered the sub up to periscope depth to investigate the noise. They rose slowly to the surface to prevent the periscope mast from causing too much turbulence in the water. Capt. Lange ordered the men to their torpedo battle stations and climbed up the conning tower to scan the horizon. He immediately yelled out *"Destroyer!"* and counted three of them roaring in for the attack. He also noted planes overhead and a possible small aircraft carrier. The *U-505* fired a T5 acoustic torpedo from a stern tube toward the distant aircraft carrier, *Guadalcanal*, and Capt. Lange ordered an emergency dive.

"There wasn't a wave in the ocean," SM2c Donald L. Carter, a signalman on board *Guadalcanal*, recalled later. *"It was calm, and the Chatelain came over the radio; it says we have a sub contact, and we're getting ready to attack. Then all hell broke loose."*

Captain Gallery was sitting on the bridge that Sunday morning, at 1110 hours, when the radio PA system announced, *"Frenchy to Bluejay (Gallery), I have a possible sound contact!"* Frenchy was Commander Knox on the USS *Chatelain* destroyer. *Chatelain's* sonar detected *U-505* about 800 yards away on her starboard bow off Cabo Blanco, Río de Oro.

Capt. Gallery jumped to his feet and gave two orders *"Left full rudder"* and *"Engines ahead full speed."* Then he grabbed the Ship Talk Mike and informed Commander Frederick S. Hall, the destroyer division commander, to take over, as he maneuvered *Guadalcanal* out of the area. Gallery wrote: *"An aircraft carrier right smack at the scene of a sound contact is like an old lady in the middle of a bar room brawl. She has no business being there, can contribute little to the work at hand, and should get the hell out of there..."* U-505, by Daniel V. Gallery, 1956, p. 262).

Capt. Gallery launched two *Wildcats*, which circled overhead like hawks. Both fighter pilots, Ensign J.W. Cadle and Lieutenant W.W. Roberts, sighted the long, dark shape of the submarine running fully submerged. They fired their 50-caliber machine guns into the water to indicate where the sub was disappearing and radioed, *"Sighted sub-destroyers head for spot where we are shooting!"*

Howard D. Sherer, the seaman on the *Guadalcanal*, recalled that their noon meal was interrupted by general quarters alarm. He raced from the chief's mess hall all the way up to his battle station on deck as a first loader for one of the ship's sixteen 40-mm cannons. The destroyers, *Pillsbury* and *Jenks*, rushed over to help *Chatelain*, as she had just run over the top of U-505. Hans Goebeler, inside the U-505, recalled that as the crew prepared to dive they heard the distinctive sound of a destroyer's propellers directly overhead.

Chatelain circled around under full rudder, maneuvered into position, and fired a salvo of twenty hedgehogs, which are small, forward-firing bombs. These projectiles fired over the bow of the ship and detonated on contact only. Captain Gallery recalled, *"All eyes locked on the spot and we ticked off each second after the splashes. When the count reached ten, we knew there was no explosion."* The target was missed. Since hedgehogs didn't explode and disturb the water, they were able to continue to track the submarine by sonar.

Hans Goebeler on U-505 recalled,

> *"Somehow the shotgun pattern of Hedgehogs missed us as we started a series of violent evasive maneuvers to throw off our attackers. We were beginning to think we might have a chance to escape when we suddenly heard a loud metallic "clinking" noise coming from above our heads.*

*Everyone in the compartment looked at each other in puzzlement, trying
to guess the meaning of such a sound...The majority opinion thought it
sounded like the links of a heavy chain being dragged across our hull,
and he feared they had snagged a mooring chain of a mine. The sound
was actually the fighter planes machine gun bullets fired to spot
the submarine."*

Using sonar to maintain contact, *Chatelain* dropped back, maneuvered into position to drop depth charges, and announced *"Contact evaluated as sub, Am starting attack."* Julian Austin, Torpedo Mate, recalled, *"We pressed the attack and set all charges for 150 feet. You can't imagine what a battle it was for each man on a K-Gun to reload with no help, while the ship was rolling and tossing."* The charges hit the water like a hand full of rocks a hundred yards ahead of where the sonar was pinpointing.

A few seconds later, *Guadalcanal* observed the ocean boil astern of the *Chatelain* as the depth charges exploded. Soon, Glenn and the men on the *Guadalcanal* and the destroyers felt the aftershock quake as a dozen geysers spouted water into the air from the underwater explosions, and cheers went up.

Goebeler, inside the *U-505*, reported that while they were still about 60-meters deep, the depth charges began to explode.

*"The first few charges were close, and the next few even closer. Then, two
ear-shattering detonations sent us flying off our feet. The boat almost
keeled over from the force of one of the blasts...the impact of those devils
was the biggest by far. All the lights went out, but we didn't need our
eyes to tell us we were taking on water in the control room...Luckily,
the leak was manageable...When the emergency lighting came on, we
tried to operate our equipment, only to discover that all electrical devices
were dead...A moment later...more bad news. Reports from the rear
compartments told of severe flooding in the aft torpedo room."*

Capt. Lange ordered the *U-505* aft torpedo room evacuated, and the watertight hatch was clamped shut. Soon the helmsman reported the sub's main rudder was jammed. The boat was out of control, turning in a tight starboard circle. Those in the control room knew the sub was plummeting toward the bottom in an uncontrolled dive. The submarine's diving planes were jammed in a downward position, with some of the ballast tank valves not responding. They desperately worked to get enough air into the tanks before they passed their crush depth. Something worked, and the sub began to slowly rise to the surface. The crew wondered if their captain would order them to "abandon ship" or to their "battle stations" to fight. They faced impossible odds in the midst of the Hunter-Killer" group supported by circling war planes. The *U-505* had no steering or diving control, no rear torpedo tubes, and a breach in the hull of the boat.

Circling in a plane above, Ensign Cadle, shouted over the radio, *"You've struck oil, Frenchy, Sub is surfacing!"* One hundred fifty miles west of Cape Blanco, French West Africa, the *U-505* heaved itself up out of the water only 700 yards from the *Chatelain*. Julian Austin reported, *"When all the charges exploded around the sub, she began to surface, not bow first like the U-515, but the conning tower broke water first in full battle trim."* As white water poured off her black sides, the *Chatelain*, *Pillsbury* and *Jenks* gunners fired at the sub with their small-caliber anti-aircraft guns. The two fighter planes strafed her decks with their 50-caliber fixed machine guns, all bullets that would not damage the submarine's pressure hull.

Goebeler of *U-505* reported:

> *"No sooner had the top of our bridge poked itself above the water than we began to hear the bell-like clang of enemy bullets slamming into our conning tower. A moment later, the heavy stuff started arriving. Our whole boat shook with the concussion of cannon shells and depth charges straddling our hull. I am not ashamed to admit that I was scared. I felt like a trapped rat."*

Hundreds of sailors, including Glenn, lined the decks of *Guadalcanal* and crowded on topside of the destroyers to watch the action. No one knew if the U-boat captain had come up to surrender or to fire a spread of torpedoes. The circling *Wildcats* flew down to strafe the sub.

As the *U-505* ran in a tight circle to the right, Captain Lange climbed up the conning tower ladder, popped open the hatch, and bravely climbed out onto the bridge amid the gunfire. He was followed by Executive Officer Paul Meyer and the bridge watch crew. Immediately, Lange was hit in the head with shrapnel torn loose by 50-caliber bullets hitting metal plates. Most of the bridge watch crew was wounded, along with Paul Meyer. Despite leg wounds, Lange crawled back to the conning tower hatch and shouted down the order to scuttle and abandon ship. Lange fell unconscious onto the bridge deck.

Pandemonium broke out below *U-505*'s deck. Goebeler reported a great mob of men from the aft end of the boat suddenly stampeded through the control room to scale the conning tower ladders. Most of the control roommates stayed at their posts to carry out the scuttling order. But they couldn't find Joseph Hauser, their Chief Engineering Officer, who was responsible for setting the demolition charges to sink the *U-505*. He had already jumped overboard. For security reasons, only three officers had the knowledge of how to arm and set the timers for the sub's 14 demolition charges. They were Engineer Hauser, Captain Lange and Executive Officer Meyer, who were already outside of the submarine.

The Engineering Petty Officer Holdenried organized a work party, which included Goebeler. They attempted to open up all the diving tanks, but the operating shafts for tanks #6 and #7 were bent from the force of the depth charges and wouldn't budge.

While the frightened crew of *U-505* was leaping into the water amid a hail of bullets, Captain Gallery broadcast to the Task Group that he wanted to capture the submarine. At 11:27 AM, Commander Hall ordered "*Cease firing.*"

As the last of the crew members made a dash for the conning tower, Goebeler, under enormous pressure, thought of the sea strainer located on the deck close to his duty station. He scrambled back, unlocked the four clamps, removed the heavy steel cover of the 12" sea strainer, opening the seacock valve. He threw the cover down onto the deck plates in the control room. A stream of water started flowing into the boat, and Goebeler rushed up the ladder onto the bridge.

Later, crew member Peter Hanson explained, "*Nobody received training or even theoretical instruction on (how to scuttle a U-boat). It was considered out of the question and totally unlikely to happen, thus the subject was entirely ignored and never even informally discussed as far as U-boats were concerned."* (p. 158, *Hunt and Kill" U-505 and the U-Boat War in the Atlantic,* by Theodore P. Savas)

By this time, the metallic clanging of bullets and shrapnel had subsided, but the shouts of wounded men continued. The whole bridge deck was tinted red with blood from the injured men. Glancing around, Goebeler observed the gray enemy destroyers and clusters of his crew mates floating in the sea, strung out in a long line behind the sub. He assisted a few other men in deploying a large inflatable life raft, and they abandoned their boat, which continued to run at about eight knots in a tight circle to the right due to a jammed rudder.

Chatelain's Captain Knox observed the submarine heading directly for his ship so he ordered a torpedo fired at it. Fortunately, it was pre-set to run at 30 feet depth and passed under the *U-505*. By now *Chatelain* had maneuvered out of the path of the submarine. Don Baker, a member of the *Guadalcanal* flight deck, observed the whole incident, and later wrote to Julian Austin,

"I will never understand why we didn't take a torpedo. No German sub was ever in a better position to torpedo a carrier. Then you (Chatelain) guys came along and spoiled U-505's plans. Thanks pal! Incidentally, your depth charges going off rang our hull like a gong. It must have really shook you up."

Away Boarders

The ancient cry of *"Away all boarding parties"* rang out over the loudspeakers. The ships of the task group prepared to drop the whaleboats into the water with their trained boarding parties. *Pillsbury* lowered her whaleboat, and in it, Lieutenant Albert L. David and his crew began to pursue the sub. They were unable to overtake the submarine, which was still making tight circles to starboard. Cutting inside the circle, *Pillsbury* pulled up alongside *U-505*, and the subs diving plane pierced a hole into *Pillsbury's* side. As a result, two main compartments, including one engine room, began to flood, and the destroyer pulled away to repair the damage.

Meanwhile, in the whaleboat, Lieutenant Albert David ordered the helmsman to execute a *"hard right rudder,"* and they intercepted the *U-505* as she completed her circle. One of the boarding party members jumped from the whaleboat onto the deck of the sub with a bowline and attached it to a cleat on the sub's deck.

Gallery reported:

> "As that tiny whaleboat took off after the circling black monster, I wouldn't have blamed those men in the boat for hoping that maybe they wouldn't catch her...cutting inside the circle the gallant band in the boat drew up alongside the runaway U-boat and leaped from the plunging whaleboat to the heaving, slippery deck. As the first one hit the deck with the whaleboat's bowline, it looked for all the world like a cowboy roping a wild horse." (Twenty Million Tons Under the Sea, Daniel V. Gallery, 1956, 2018, p. 234).

This boarding marked the first capture of an enemy warship by the U.S. Navy since 1815. But the U-505 was sinking and the entire back part, known as the stern, was under water. God only knew what was below the deck; were there armed men ready to defend the boat or demolition charges ticking away? No one in the boarding party had ever been on a submarine of any kind before, and this one was a runaway German sub. Without hesitation, Lieutenant David, Torpedo-man-Arthur K. Knispel, and Radioman-Stanley E. Wdowiak climbed the ladder to the conning tower bridge where they found a dead German crew member lying face down.

The men descended the conning tower hatch of U-505 into the semi-darkness, amid a mysterious array of pipes, levers, valves, and instruments with German labels. Ready to fight anyone left on board, each man carried a Thompson submachine gun. Finding no one below, they quickly went to work closing valves. Hans Goebeler reported, "Climbing down through that hatch into the dark conning tower of a sinking enemy submarine is the most heroic act I've ever heard of." David later said he knew how Jonah in the Bible felt on his way down into the belly of the whale.

Knispel and Wdowiak ran forward to get the codebooks from the radio room. They forced open the locker, bagged the books and Enigma machine and passed them up to the deck, along with guns and binoculars.

Lt. David yelled up to the deck for more of the boarding party members to crawl down and help. Ultimately, nine men went down the hatch, while three men stayed with the whale boat. One of the first to enter the U-boat was Zenon B. Lukosius, known as Luke. He immediately heard the flow of water entering the control room from the open sea chest. He frantically searched for and found the cover lying in water on the floor plates. Luke quickly replaced the cover to stop the incoming flow of sea water.

Goebeler later regretted not throwing the sea strainer cover down into the bilge, where it could not have been retrieved. He also reported that what Luke and the other American sailors did to salvage *U-505* was the very definition of bravery.

The U-boat was so low in the water now that the waves began to wash down the conning tower hatch. David ordered the man left on deck to close the hatch while they continued to work below. At this time, the main electric motors were still propelling the submarine in a circle at about six knots.

Meanwhile, the *Wildcat* airplanes that had assisted in the attack landed back on the *Guadalcanal*, and Gallery ordered the *Chatelain* and *Jenks* to pick up the survivors. German prisoner, Hans Goebeler, later wrote,

> "While we bobbed in the surf, we watched with amusement as the Americans chased our still-circling boat with motorized whaleboats. Eventually they managed to board her, but we were still confident it was only a matter of time before she slipped beneath the waves. After all, only a sliver of her bow and conning tower was still above water."

Lieutenant David and his boarding men, including Gunner Burr, searched for and found thirteen of the sub's fourteen unarmed demolition charges. About an hour after the boarding party from *Pillsbury* entered the U-boat, Gallery ordered his Chief Engineer, Commander Earl Trosino, to lead *Guadalcanal's* group of "experts" over to the sub in two whaleboats. *Guadalcanal's* boarding parties scrambled to their awaiting whaleboats and were lowered into the water.

Glenn Peter Larson was a member of Boarding Boat #3 at 12:58 P.M. on motor whaleboat No. 2's initial trip. There were seventeen members of this boarding party and three boat crew members.

Ten minutes after departure, one of the boats was picked up by a wave and deposited on the deck of the sub with a bang. The sound of the crash caused some concern for those below deck, who had no idea what was happening. Comdr. Trosino and his crew from *Guadalcanal* scrambled across the deck of *U-505* and up to the bridge, but they couldn't open the hatch due to a vacuum inside the sub.

Capt. Gallery reported that the circling U-boat was constantly passing Germans in their rubber boats, so several of Trosino's men grabbed a survivor, hauled him aboard and asked him how to open the hatch. He showed them a little valve which let air into the pressure hull to equalize it, and this enabled the sailors to open the hatch.

Comdr. Trosino then climbed down the hatch and took over command of the *U-505* from Lieutenant David. The *Pillsbury* came alongside to deliver salvage pumps and to place a tow line on the *U-505*. The destroyer came too close to the sub, and unfortunately, *U-505's* diving plane pierced the *Pillsbury's* hull, flooding engineering space B-2. The destroyer was then forced to back off to repair the damage.

Only U-505's bow and conning tower was still above the water during capture.

At 2:15 P.M. the *Guadalcanal* came alongside the *U-505* at a safe distance and Trosino pulled switches to stop the sub's engine. At a stop, the submarine lost the lift of her stern diving planes, settled to a steeper angle and submerged the conning tower hatch. The carrier crew quickly threw a 1-1/4-inch wire towline over to the sub's boarding party.

During this brief time, the *Guadalcanal's* stern was about 50 feet from the snout of the sub, with its four loaded torpedo tubes pointed right at the carrier. Capt. Gallery prayed *"Dear Lord, I've got a bunch of inquisitive young lads on that submarine. Please don't let any of them monkey with the firing switch."* (*Saturday Evening Post*, August 4, 1945)

When the towline was securely fastened, *Guadalcanal* moved ahead and the *U-505's* stern came up, along with the spirits of the whole Task Force. But the U-boats rudder was still jammed hard right, causing the sub to shear out on the starboard side of the carrier. On the *Chatelain*, 500 yards away, the forty surviving prisoners looked on with shock and disbelief as they watched their captured submarine in tow.

Now the hatch was opened again and with both excitement and trepidation, several men, including Glenn climbed below deck. Fear and heroism usually intersect, and the boarding parties immediately went to work closing valves and water-tight doors, rigging gasoline-driven billy pumps, and assisting with the removal of official-looking German papers. Trosino spent the next couple of hours in the bilges tracing pipes and studying the operation of the engines.

While searching below deck on the U-boat, Glenn discovered an interesting German pistol. He visualized it as an impressive souvenir, but none of the men were able to keep anything they found during their search.

Capt. Gallery sent a coded message to Washington requesting immediate assistance to tow the captured *U-505* and a U. S. flag was hung on the sub's bridge. *Guadalcanal* recovered two *Avengers* and two *Wild Cats* that were running low on fuel. Traveling at only six knots, Gallery was concerned the Task Group would be sitting ducks for an enemy U-boat. Without hesitation, he launched an *Avenger* to carry the *U-505* code books and Enigma machine to Gibraltar, which were then flown to London. Running low on fuel, Gallery sent a dispatch requesting orders to head for the nearest friendly port, which was Dakar.

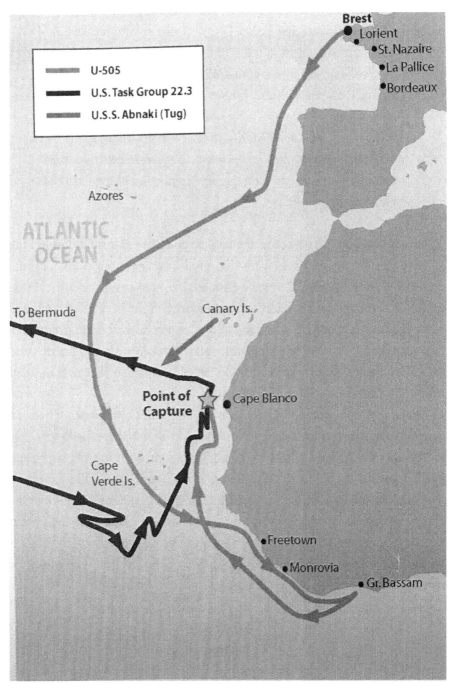

U-505 *capture*

The prisoners who were herded on the destroyer earlier were now transferred to the *Guadalcanal* by breeches buoys. *U-505's* Goebeler later recalled:

> *"We were happy-happy-happy to be alive! We believed we had done our duty and put down our share of enemy shipping, and now were one of the few U-boat crews to survive the sinking of their own ship...Several of our crew had been wounded during our evacuation of the boat, and they were given immediate medical treatment. The more seriously wounded were taken to the sick bay, including our skipper Harald Lane who had to have his leg amputated."*

Miraculously, there was only one fatality on either side, and once on the aircraft carrier, the prisoners were showered with seawater to wash off the diesel oil that had leaked from the U-boat. The POWs were held in a large cage-like compartment located right below the flight deck. Heat radiated from the carrier's engine exhausts, and Glenn recalled hearing them call for *"das Wasser"* (water). An American sailor hooked up a fan on them to help alleviate the relentless heat, and Goebeler reported that overall, *"Our treatment at the hands of the Americans was fairly good."*

At 7:16 P.M., *Guadalcanal's* Can Do boarding parties were brought back on board, along with hundreds of confidential documents from the *U-505*.

The Task Group turned into the wind, landed their air patrol planes, and headed toward Dakar, Northwest Africa. A few hours later, Gallery received a message from the Commander-in-Chief of the U.S. Atlantic Fleet that fuel and a tug boat were on their way and Gallery was directed to make port at Casablanca with the Task Group. Washington intelligence knew that Dakar was full of enemy spies and that the news of the capture would quickly reach Germany.

Towing Troubles

That same night, Capt. Gallery received orders to take his prize to Bermuda, instead of Dakar. Admiral Ingersoll, Commander of the U.S.

Atlantic fleet, diverted the fleet tug *"Abnaki"* from an eastbound convoy to take over the towing of the *U-505*, and the oiler *"Kennebeck"* was also on its way to refuel the task group.

Glenn recalled that around midnight on June 4-5, the 1-1/4 inch wire towline to the *U-505* broke. Under a full moon, the destroyer escort ships circled the now free sub, and Gallery put up air patrol for the rest of the night.

The next morning, June 5, 1944, the *Guadalcanal* came alongside the *U-505* and passed a stronger 2 1/4-inch wire towline. Comander Trosino felt he could move the rudder by the hand-steering gear in the after-torpedo room. But it appeared the door to the compartment had a booby trap. Gallery was itching to visit the sub, so he and Trosino took four helpers and went over to the *U-505* to investigate. They scrambled up on the bridge and closed the conning tower hatch behind them as they entered the sub. The boat was way down by the stern and wallowing in the water.

This was Gallery's first time on a submarine, and since the battery was low, the lights burned very dimly, and the air stunk. Using his flashlight, Trosino led the way and pointed the light at an open fuse box full of exposed fuses and many wires leading in and out. Gallery eased the cover shut and nothing happened. Next, they carefully dialed open the hatch; no water. So they swung open the door and scrambled aft to the hand steering gear. In less than a minute, Trosino moved the rudder back amidship (middle). They were now able to proceed at eight knots, with the sub towing along behind properly.

Meanwhile on June 4-5 in Europe, Glenn's brother, Duane, was busy straffng the German coastal fortifications along the French coast with his P-51 to encourage the Germans to move inland. It was in preparation for the Invasion of Normandy the following day. Back on the farm at Regent, North Dakota, the boys' parents went about their daily chores, blissfully unaware of the historic events and dangers in which their sons were participating in during the fight against evil. As the psalmist reminds us, *"God is our refuge and strength, a very present help in trouble. Therefore, we will not fear, though the earth give way, and the mountains fall into the heart of the sea, though its waters roar and foam, and the mountains quake with their surging...Be still, and know that I am God."* (Psalm 46:1,10) The same full moon and celestial stars shown over all of them that night.

On June 9, 1944, *Abnaki* and *Kennebeck* rendezvoused with Gallery's Task Group at sea. The tug took over towing "Junior," as the crew nicknamed the *U-505*, and the tanker refueled the ships. Captain Gallery now headed his Task Group for Bermuda, 2,500 miles away.

Upon arrival at the Bermuda harbor on June 19, the *U-505* was camouflaged with black paint, renamed the USS *Nemo*, and hidden under heavy guard for the remainder of the war. The submarine's two acoustically guided torpedoes were taken so the Allies could study how the new mechanism worked.

Gallery turned 59 German prisoners of war over to the Commandant of the Naval Operations Base at Bermuda. The POWs were later transferred to a prison camp in Ruston, Louisiana. To conceal the capture of *U-505*, American authorities did not inform the International Red Cross of their survival, and they were denied mail service. Imagine the anguish their families went through when Germany assumed the *U-505* was lost at sea. When the war was over, they were allowed to contact their families by mail. Eventually, three of the men resettled in the United States. While *Guadalcanal* was in bay at Bermuda, the men played volleyball on one of the elevators and baseball on shore, where Gallery hit a home run. After the game, the ship held a swim call, and the sailors cooled off in the Atlantic.

As Gallery's Hunter-Killer Task Group steamed toward Norfolk, the U.S. was engaged in the Battle of Saipan in the Pacific, and the U.S. Army was advancing into Europe through France. Glenn's brother, Duane, later wrote: "*I was on another mission to Berlin here awhile back. It was clear as a bell, and we could see the whole city. We flew right through the flak and dropped our droppable wing tanks right over the city.*"

Task Group 22.3 cruised into Norfolk on June 22, 1944, for repairs and alterations with one of the best kept secrets of World War II. Glenn journaled, "*Arrived at Norfolk, Virginia; received 15 days' leave and went home to North Dakota*" to meet Clara.

CHAPTER 17

Engaged and Hospitalized

CLARA'S HEART BEAT WITH EXCITEMENT AS she read Glenn's telegram, *"Meet me in North Dakota, Darling. I am coming home on leave."* The railroad station in San Diego bustled with wartime activity, and sailors were coming and going.

As the train chugged along, Glenn periodically checked on the diamond ring he carried safely in his pocket. It seemed like the journey to North Dakota took forever. And he had to remember that he couldn't leak any hint of information about the exciting capture of the *U-505*.

Their time together at Regent was sweet, exciting, romantic, and bittersweet. Clara's father, Chris Schweigert, was impressed that Glenn had asked him for permission to marry his daughter.

Glenn's mother, Lillie, cooked his favorite foods, and some of his friends stopped in to visit the couple. Raymond was busy with farm work, and Glenn eagerly helped him as he could.

One warm evening, Glenn took Clara for a drive by the lake and, perhaps under a canopy of stars, he presented her with the diamond ring he had promised. She was elated. The wedding would depend on when Glenn would return from the war. He wished he could tell her about his dangerous adventure of boarding a nearly submerged U-boat just three weeks prior, but he didn't. Time passed too quickly. A war-time romance was difficult and emotional. As they parted each to return to a different coast, Clara thought Glenn's skin had a yellowish, golden glow to it.

Glenn was fatigued on the train and ill by the time he returned to Norfolk on July 8, 1944. The next day, the Navy doctor examined him and diagnosed hepatitis, which was commonly known as "yellow jaundice." It is an inflammation of the liver and can cause flu like symptoms. Glenn was admitted that day to Portsmouth Naval Hospital for medical treatment. He later wondered if he had possibly contracted hepatitis from the water he drank from the goatskin bag in Morocco?

While hospitalized, his ship departed without him on July 15, for its Fourth ASW Cruise. The *Guadalcanal* performed training exercises at Bermuda, and perhaps they peeked in on the *U-505*, which was hidden at a dock nearby.

In the middle of July, Glenn's father wrote a letter to North Dakota Senator William Langer. He requested assistance from him to bring Glenn back home for his rehabilitation. He wondered if Glenn could be entitled to sick leave that could possibly be extended for a while into the harvest. The Navy denied his request.

When stable, Glenn was transferred to the U.S. Naval Hospital at Brooklyn, New York, for medical treatment as his liver healed, and his rehabilitation continued. He journaled, *"August 1, entered Rockefeller Institute Hospital in New York City."* He had lost considerable weight, but gradually his appetite returned, and his bilirubin blood level fell. His rehab even included an outing to the Brooklyn Zoo, where he watched and laughed as one of the apes threw rotten apples at visitors.

On September 5, Glenn and two other men were discharged from the hospital for transfer back to Norfolk via Baltimore, Maryland. They rode the train in 1st Class Staterooms accompanied by a deputy. Fortunately, his ship was back in Norfolk port for repairs and alterations, and Glenn journaled on September 7, *"I am back aboard the trusty Guadalcanal."*

On September 16, Admiral Reed, Commander-in-Chief, U.S. Atlantic Fleet presented Glenn and the other submarine boarders the following Citation, *"For heroic and meritorious service, the nature of which cannot be revealed at the time. A copy of this citation is to be made part of the official record of G.P. Larson, and he is hereby authorized to wear the Commendation Ribbon."*

That same day, Captain Gallery was relieved of Command of *Guadalcanal*, and replaced by Captain B.C. McCaffree, USN. Gallery was later awarded the Navy Distinguished Service Medal for the daring exploit.

CHAPTER 18

Hurricane During the Fifth ASW Cruise

Eternal Father, Strong to Save by William Whiting, 1860

Eternal Father, strong to save,
Whose arm has bound the restless wave,
Who bids the mighty ocean deep
Its own appointed limits keep:
Oh, hear us when we cry to Thee
For those in Peril on the sea.

THE TASK GROUP DEPARTED NORFOLK, VIRGINIA, for the open Atlantic and Cape Verde Islands on September 28, 1944. The Destroyer Escort ships *Pillsbury, Pope, Flaherty, Chatelain, and Neuner* accompanied the *Guadalcanal*. A week later, Glenn was pleased to be awarded Electrician's Mate First Class.

In the next couple weeks, two U-boats were detected, but the Task Group's attacks on them were unsuccessful. The new captain ventured further north past England and up around Iceland. The weather grew worse, and two aircraft crash landed on October 11. Six days later, they were in gale and hurricane weather. Waves were exceedingly high in the morning and increased to mountainous size in the afternoon. The wind averaged 55 miles per hour, with gusts as high as 80 mph. The crew was experiencing one of the North Atlantic Storms, which are known to be the most fierce in the world.

Donald M. Baker, an Aviation Boatswain's Mate, 1st Class, worked on the flight deck of the *Guadalcanal*, helping launch and recover the ship's aircraft. He recorded his story of The Big Storm:

"By the 16 of October we had reached Latitude 57 deg, 57 min North, and Longitude 34 deg, 26 min West, which was about as far north as the ship

had ever sailed. That morning, the wind was building, and gusts to 56 knots were measured. Dark scudding clouds obscured the sun and, by noon, it looked like night and we secured from flight operations.

The noon meal was to prove an unforgettable experience. The ship was rolling hard. Down in the mess hall, we went through the chow line and, carefully balancing mess trays, made our way to a seat at the tables...It was really funny at first. As the ship rolled, every man would hold one end of his tray, picking it up so as to keep the tray level, while forking food with the other hand. As the roll to the other side started, everyone quickly switched hands, and the operation was repeated. Actually, you could eat pretty good once you got the timing figured out and the meal was progressing in good shape.

Then a roll to port began that felt like it would never end. As everyone hung on for dear life, one of the mess tables collapsed. Men, table, and benches went hurling across the deck to smash into the opposite bulkhead. On the opposite roll, they all came skidding back on a deck now well greased with mashed potatoes and gravy, jello, hot coffee and salad greens. Picking up speed, men, tables, benches, and food crashed into the tables on the other side causing more tables to collapse. What started out as merely funny was fast becoming pretty serious. The laughing turned to curses, mixed with groans. Everyone was down on the deck now on hands and knees, and it was almost impossible to stand up. As a table and its load of men came shooting across the deck, those on the other side scrambled frantically trying to get out of the way. All the tables came down, and people were getting bruised as they slammed into the bulkheads. The deck was covered with men, overturned tables and benches, and the whole mess liberally covered with spilled food.

Those of us who had come down from the flight deck decided it would be a damn site safer topside. Extracting ourselves from the tangled mess as fast as possible, we headed for "safety" topside. After this fiasco, the mess hall and galley were secured for the next three days, and we lived on *sandwiches and coffee. A few hands reported to sick bay for treatment of assorted bumps and bruises."*

The storm continued to build for the next two days. The quartermasters were holding 20 to 30 degrees of rudder trying to keep the ship on base course. The storm was a spectacular sight from up on the flight deck. The waves were huge. Green water was coming over the flight deck 60 feet above the water line. The ship was rolling so hard we had to double-up on the aircraft tie-down lines and, even at that, with the lines stretched to the limit, it appeared some of those airplanes would snap the lines and slide into the catwalks. The wind was blowing so hard aircraft propellers were actually turning in the wind; not spinning, but hitching around in little jerks. Ordinarily, it took two men pulling hard on a propeller tip to turn one of those engines over."

The ship would struggle to rise on the crest of a wave only to fall off into a trough, and the only sight was mountainous waves all around higher than the deck. Nosing into a wave, the bow would begin to rise, water cascading off the deck. Stuck on the face of a huge wave, the ship would come to a halt and slide backwards, completely burying the 5-inch gun mount on the fantail. The vibration caused by the ship sliding backward against the thrust of the propellers shook the hull like a dog with a bone in its teeth. The expansion joints in the flight deck were gaping far beyond anything seen before as the hull was wracked by the waves. The combination of the wind and rolling made it impossible to move around: we were just too busy hanging on.

The Destroyers were having a rough time of it, also. They were cocky little ships and good company for the business we were in. As we watched from the catwalks, a DE would nose into a wave and go out of sight with just a bit of the bridge and the radar mast sticking out. As we stood watching and wondering if they would ever come up again, the wave would roll on by, and the little ship would come rearing up, the water cascading off her decks, only to repeat the process with the next wave. Those guys should

*have been drawing submarine pay; they were under the waves as much
as they were on top."*

*Down on the hangar deck, the side plates between the flight deck and
hangar deck began to fail. Huge cracks in the plates would open and
close as the hull wracked and twisted. When the edges of a crack would
momentarily close up, a ship fitter would throw a fast tack on it with his
welding rod hoping to pin the crack, but it was a losing proposition. On
the next heave of the hull, the weld would let go with a loud crack, and
the tear would continue on up the plate. Water began spurting through
the cracks onto the deck.*

*The storm continued the next day building in intensity. Wind gusts were
reaching 75 knots, and waves were estimated to be about 60 feet high.
Finally, the hangar deck doors off the fantail gave way, and water began
washing in on the hangar deck. The aft elevator pit flooded and filled
with seawater like a swimming pool.*

*Sleep was hard to come by. The rolling was so intense we had to strap
ourselves into the bunks to keep from being tossed out. This storm lasted
for three days. The Task Group could do nothing but ride it out. Finally,
by noon the third day, the wind began to abate and the seas moderate.
It was a time to take stock of our situation. It turned out considerable
damage had been done. The hull had cracked and admitted seawater to
the boiler feed water tanks. The feed water was now contaminated and
could not be used to make steam. The ship was forced to run on what
water could be made with the evaporators, and the engines demands
came first. Fresh water was in short supply. Seawater was supplied to the
heads, and we had our first experience showering in salt water. It wasn't
too bad if you dried quickly so the water didn't leave salt deposits on the
skin. Of more concern was the drinking water. The scuttlebutts were
turned off except for ten minutes every hour. The galley was still shut
down, and sandwiches began to get tiresome, but no one had
to go hungry."*

BEVERLY LARSON CHRISTENSEN   99

Julian Austin, who turned 96 in May 2021, was on the *Chatalain*. He recalled, "*The Destroyer Escorts, being much smaller ships, were experiencing severe difficulties. Roll indicators showed 50 degrees...At more than one point we expected the ship to just break in two and that would have been the end of all of us*". Austin said they could turn to go into the wind, but the larger *Guadalcanal* carrier couldn't complete the turn into the fierce south wind. So the destroyers had to turn around and go with the carrier and wind.

After the storm subsided, Don Baker of the *Guadalcanal* noted:

> "*Some life rafts had been swept away, and the anchor windlass electrical circuits were out. It appeared the 5" gun mound was damaged, and the hangar deck bulkhead doors to the fantail needed repairing. There were numerous cracks in the hull and flight deck structures but, by late that afternoon, the ship was able to resume flight operations, and we headed for Ponta Delgada (Azores in Portugal), arriving on the 30th of October. After refueling, we headed back to Norfolk, where the ship went into dry dock for a month of repairs, and the crew went ashore for a little rest and relaxation.*"

In an October 2008 telephone interview with Glenn's shipmate friend, Richard DeMarco, Electrician Mate 1C, told the following story:

> "*During a storm at sea, Glenn and I were sitting around the communication room, and the ship was rocking back and forth. We thought we ought to suspend the coffee pot and record player from the ceiling, and it worked. Whenever the ship rocked, they would swing way out one way and then the other way. So we had coffee and music during the storm. When a Division Officer entered the room, he said, 'My God, I've seen everything now!'*"

Glenn recalled that during the big storm, the flight deck would raise up to 15 feet on one end with each gigantic wave. He later told Clara that he thought he would never see her again.

But he did.

CHAPTER 19

A Wartime Wedding

Glenn's brother, Duane, was flying out of Fowlmere, England in October, 1944, with the 504th Fighter Squadron, 339th Fighter Group. He wrote the following:

> "It's pretty damp over here in the winter time. There's always a warm or a cold front moving in or out, which to a pilot means lots of instruments. I'm hoping to be home by Christmas time, but I can't be sure until the time comes when I actually start home. The tour over here has been lowered to 270 hours now and I've got about 248. If they accept the request I put in, when my tour is finished, I'll get a thirty day leave at home and then come back to this same outfit for another tour. I will also get promoted to Captain before I come home. My Flight Leader finished up and went home about two weeks ago and I was the Assistant Flight Leader, so now I am the Flight Leader...Right now I am making about $325 a month.
>
> I was in on another mission to Berlin here awhile back. It was clear as a bell so we could see the whole city. We flew right through the flak and dropped our droppable wing tanks right over the city from about 25,000 feet."

The following month, Glenn journaled, "*Received 16 days' leave, married to Miss Clara Schweigert of Stanton, North Dakota, November 13, 1944, at San Diego, California.*" He eagerly boarded a train and traveled nearly 3,000 miles to Coronado to marry Clara. Six people were present at the church, the pastor, the pianist, Glenn and Clara and their two witnesses, her sister Helene, and neighbor, Velma Kraft.

During their brief honeymoon, they drove to Los Angeles to visit Glenn's grandmother, Minnie Schow; her sister, Carrie Noben; and his uncle, Robbie Schow, and wife. Clara was so appreciative of Robbie's wife, Helene, for arranging a professional wedding photograph of them while they were there.

It was an emotional time for them, with the uncertainty of the war. The days passed quickly, and it was difficult to say goodbye. After another three-day train ride, Glenn, wearing his Navy uniform, reported back to duty at Norfolk, Virginia. Clara's father was disappointed that they were not able to attend the wedding, and wrote the following letter to her:

Clara and Glenn's wedding photograph

"MERCER COUNTY
COUNTY JUDGE
STANTON, N. DAK.
November 21, 1944

Dear Clara,

*Yours and Glenn's letters just arrived this morning, and I don't want
to put off writing to you as I may not get the time, so first of all I want
to extend Ma's and my best wishes and congratulations to both of you.
May God protect and keep both of you in these fateful days and make it
possible for you to live a long and happy life together."*

*The telegram kind of took us off our feet, as we had hoped we would have
a little advance notice and, if I had known in time, I might have even
made the trip out there by air, but we realize that you could not tell just
when Glenn would get there, so the best we can hope for now is a happy
reunion when it's over over there....I met Geneva and Mildred on the train
Thursday and told them about your marriage and you should have seen
them. They went right up in the air. I got a kick out of how excited they got.
The Wilson girls were on the train, too, and thought their father had told
them of the telegram, but they didn't know anything about it either.*

*Again, wishing you all the happiness in the world and that you will be
united with Glenn before too long. I remain as ever, Your loving Father.
P.S. Send me Glenn's address so I can drop him a line, too.*

Love, Dad"

At the same time that Clara's father was writing his letter to the
newlyweds, the US Army was advancing through northern France
toward Germany. Regent native, Robert Goodwin Larson, was among
the soldiers serving there, and two days prior to Thanksgiving 1944 he
was shot in the foot while running a message to the front line. He had

Clara's parents, Regina and Christian Schweigert

surgery in Mericourt, France, recovered in England, and was awarded a Purple Heart.

The next month in December of 1944, Hitler launched a surprise attack through Belgium to split the British Army in the North and the American Army in the South. The U.S. suffered over 80,000 casualties, but the line did not break. Albert Dobitz of Regent was an Infantryman and earned a Bronze Star and Purple Heart during the Battle of the Bulge.

CHAPTER 20

Guadalcanal's Seventh Cruise

GLENN PENNED, "*DECEMBER 25, 1944, PULLED into Guantanemo Bay in Cuba for a month's stay.*" Another Christmas without snow or family, but the crew was served a fine holiday meal in the mess hall.

The night before, on Christmas Eve, over 2,000 American soldiers were transported across the English Channel on the *Leopoldville* as reinforcements in the fierce Battle of the Bulge in Germany. The troopship was torpedoed by *U-486* and sank two and a half hours later. Regent native, Pfc. Allan J. Dorgan, 22, died in the water there that night, along with 763 other Americans. It was

Glenn's souveneir Cruise Album

the worst tragedy ever to an American Infantry Division as the result of an enemy submarine attack.

On New Year's Day, 1945, Glenn passed around his souvenir leather-bound scrapbook for friends to sign. Richard DeMarco, from American Fork, Utah, signed "*Pistol packing Pete* (Glenn's nickname), *may our friendship never cease.*" W.L. Stein, EM 1C of Marysville, California, wrote, "*Remember New York.*" He was in the same boarding party as Glenn during the *U-505* capture. S.S. Shepard was the Chief Electrician on the USS *Guadalcanal*.

Glenn's diary continued, "*February 1, 1945 Navy shipyard at Portsmouth, Virginia, for repairs.*" After the extensive damage from the Big Storm, the *Guadalcanal* was never used in battle again, but rather for pilot training.

Autogpraphs inside Glenn's Cruise Album

CHAPTER 21

Eighth ASW Cruise

March 1, 1945, Glenn wrote, *"Back to Cuba for another week."* That day a horrific accident occurred on the flight deck, and it greatly disturbed Glenn and the other men. Donald Baker, ABH1C, wrote the following:

"Seaman first class Jack Sargent was a member of the ship's flight deck crew. During the previous night's operations, he had been fatally injured in a terrible accident. One of the landing cables had snapped as a TBM aircraft landed. A piece of the severed cable caught him across the legs as he stood on the flight deck.

For the burial at sea, all available personnel were mustered on the hangar deck in dress uniforms to pay our last respects to one of ours. An American flag covered the body, which was encased in a weighted canvas shroud and sewn tight. The flag-covered boy rested at one end of a long, wide wooden platform, which extended out over the water.

After the Captain's eulogy and prayer, the honor guard snapped to Attention and fired their salute. Somewhere faintly, I heard a dog, a small one, barking far off in the bowels of the ship. The board tilted, and the canvas-cased body slid down the board into the sea with a soft scraping sound so distinct I have never forgotten it."

March 13, 1945, Glenn wrote to Clara, *"I can hardly wait to hold you in my arms again...Your loving sailor, Glenn."* That same day, half way around the world in the Pacific theatre, Glenn's high school classmate, Corporal Clifford Newby, was busy dodging shells in the Philippines, and Michael G. Greff, of Regent, was wounded, for which he received a Purple Heart.

Just five months prior, his brother, Godfrey Greff, aboard the USS *Raymond* Destroyer Escort, participated in the heavy Battle near Samar during the Battle of Leyte Gulf. The largest naval battle of WWII, with over 200,000 naval personnel involved, was decisive and crippled the Japanese Combined Fleet, permitting U.S. invasion of the Philippines. Five U.S. ships were sunk, but the USS *Raymond* survived the battle, picked up survivors from the carrier *St. Lou*, and was later awarded a Presidential Citation.

Guadalcanal pilot qualifications continued with one aircraft crash in March and three on the 5th of April, 1945. The first two were into the catwalk, and in the third, the pilot escaped as the aircraft burst into flames. On April 15, the carrier moved to Jacksonville, Florida, to continue training Navy and Marine pilots.

Death of a President and Victory in Europe

The Allies had captured the industrial heart of Germany by early April, and many cities were in rubble from Allied bombing raids. When many Nazi soldiers began to put down their arms in mass surrender, Hitler's SS hunted them down and hanged them from lampposts. On April 16, Hitler's birthday, American troops reached Nuremberg, where massive Nazi Party rallies had been held and Hitler gave some of his wildest speeches. The Nazis now enlisted the Hitler Youth, boys as young as 15, to fight on the front lines.

As the Allies pushed across Germany, they liberated more than 100 concentration camps. Even Lieutenant General George S. Patton became physically sick from the sights and smell as he toured Ohrdurf concentration camp with Eisenhower on April 12, 1945.

A few hours later, the radio announcement of President Franklin D. Roosevelt's death at age 63 stunned the world. He had been under tremendous pressure during the war, and his declining physical health had been kept a secret from the general public. His Vice-President, Harry S. Truman, now became Commander-in-Chief.

The Allies were now 50 miles from Berlin, but Eisenhower halted their advance, so that the Soviets could capture Berlin for themselves. The Red Army sustained more than 300,000 casualties in the battle for Berlin. Months earlier, at the Yalta Conference, Roosevelt, Winston Churchill and Joseph Stalin had agreed to Soviet postwar occupation of Berlin.

Hitler had vowed to never see Germany surrender as it did in World War I. On April 30, as bombs dropped above his Berlin bunker, he and his wife, Eva, committed suicide. Hitler had left Karl Donitz in charge and four days later, Donitz broadcast a Cease Fire order to all U-boat commanders. The war had been devastating to the 38,000 young men who served in Germany's U-boat fleet, as some 30,000 were killed in action.

Berlin fell to the invading Russian armies on May 3, and, that same day, *Guadalcanal* arrived at Mayport, Florida, for replenishment. Glenn received transfer orders and 30 days' leave. He proceeded to Norfolk, where he met Clara. She was accompanied on the long train ride from California by Bonnie, (Mrs. M.G.), Langford, whose husband was also in Glenn's *U-505* boarding party.

Nazi Germany surrendered to the Allies on May 7, 1945, and the next day, when surrender was signed with the Soviets, was Victory in Europe. What wonderful news! Glenn declared it to be one of the happiest days of his life. Now only Japan remained undefeated.

A Delayed Wedding Reception

Glenn and Clara joyfully traveled home to North Dakota to visit their parents. Glenn helped Raymond with spring's work, which included seeding that year's crop and milking the cows.

Lillie arranged a wedding reception for Glenn and Clara with family and friends at their farm. That evening in May 1945, Raymond and Lillie hosted a Wedding Dance at the Woodman Hall in Regent. Clara remembered that her in-laws were excellent dancers, but for Glenn, dancing was a life-long agony. Amos Tollefson, a family friend asked the bride for a dance, and as they waltzed along, he confided in her that Glenn was about the most honest

Wedding reception   *Wedding reception at the Larson farm.*
                                   Clara, Glenn, Lillie and Raymond

person he knew. It was a comforting thought for the bride. The merriment continued long into the night.

The newlyweds also spent some time with Clara's parents at Stanton, North Dakota. At breakfast, Glenn's father-in-law looked up from his newspaper and said, "What do you know about the *U-505*?" Glenn's face turned pale as he thought someone leaked the secret. But Christian reassured him that he had just read the news about the capture of the U-boat in the *Bismarck Tribune*. Since the war with Germany was over, it was no longer classified information.

Now only Japan continued to fight. They wondered where Glenn's transfer would take him; time would tell.

Under command of the author, a prize crew from the Escort Carrier USS Guadalcanal *(in background)* swarms over the German U-boat 505—the first time in our history since 1815 that a foreign enemy man-of-war has been boarded and captured on the high seas.

We Captured a German Sub

By Capt. D. V. GALLERY, USN

One of the best-kept secrets of the war is now revealed—the commanding officer's own story of a battle without parallel in American naval history.

THE story of this battle, without parallel in American naval history, really begins on April ninth of last year, when the task group I commanded was making its first antisubmarine cruise near the Azores. The action seems to me all the more remarkable because all the ships of the task group—the baby flattop Guadalcanal and her five escort destroyers, the Pillsbury, Pope, Chatelain, Flaherty and Jenks—were less than a year old and 80 per cent of the crews were landlubbers from our inland farms and cities, serving on their first seagoing vessel. Fools rush in? Well, maybe.

During that first cruise, our task group engaged in a long game of hide and seek with an ace of the U-boat fleet, Kapitän Leutnant Werner Henke—Knight's Cross of the Iron Cross, with Oak Leaves—in the U-515. After the Guadalcanal's planes from VC Squadron 58 did their spotting job, the destroyers got on the scent, tracking the deeply submerged U-boat by sound indications. The U-515 was brought to the surface with depth charges in the middle of a group of three cans. The sub surfaced in perfect position to sink one or more of our destroyers by torpedoes or gunfire before she was hammered to pieces. But she made only a feeble effort to fight. The U-515's crew swarmed on deck and leaped overboard as fast as possible. We poured rockets and shells into the sub for five minutes before she upended and sank.

After we picked up Henke and survivors of his crew, it struck us that here was an ace of the U-boat fleet, a man of proved courage and skill, yet when cornered he didn't fight. He didn't blow up his boat. He and his crew of veterans, with him for two years, abandoned ship in confusion. The startling conclusion was that if we had ceased firing and had called away boarding parties immediately, we might have boarded and captured the U-515. Of course, the call "Away, boarders!" had never been used in any modern navy—boarding parties went out of fashion 100 years ago with the advent of long-range guns.

But there was the fact staring us in the face: If we had had sufficient imagination to foresee our opportunity and be set for it, we might have made modern naval history. We determined then and there to be set the next time. So, before our next cruise, at a conference in Norfolk attended by the commanding officers of all vessels of the task group, we agreed to make capture our objective. All ships were directed to organize boarding parties and prize crews, and to draw plans for capturing and towing a submarine.

We decided that if we brought a sub to the surface we would immediately stop firing weapons that could sink her, such as torpedoes, depth charges or armor-piercing shells. We would encourage the crew to abandon the sub by smothering her with fire from small weapons. At the time we drew up this plan, I'm

sure most of us thought it was visionary—shooting the moon. But anyway, the boarding parties were organized and instructed.

We sailed on May fifteenth of last year with orders to operate west of the Cape Verde Islands. Hunting submarines is big-game hunting, but 99 per cent of the time it is a most monotonous and discouraging occupation. Your planes scour the ocean continuously, day and night. The gun crews practically live at their stations. For a month at a time nothing may happen except perhaps a false alarm or two, when the lads get desperate and begin imagining things. Then, just about the time you decide that there are no submarines in the ocean, all hell busts loose.

When you do pick up a hot trail, and know it's the McCoy, the news goes through the ship like an electric shock. All hands know that from then on they are playing for keeps.

The sub is a wily quarry. Her lookouts know their lives depend on alertness, and so, more often than not, they spot your planes in time to give warning for a

Captain Gallery, leader of the force that snatched the scuttled U-boat from Davy Jones's locker.

The Saturday Evening Post, *August 4, 1945*

CHAPTER 22

Transfer to USS *Namakagon* Tanker

CLARA RETURNED TO NORFOLK WITH GLENN as he thought he would probably be transferred to New York. He was disappointed when he received orders on June 11 to report to New Orleans, Louisiana, for duty on the USS *Namakagon*. The gasoline tanker was built by Cargill in Savage, Minnesota, one of 22 ships built there.

Prior to WW II, Cargill, Inc. was known for building large barges to haul grain. In order to accommodate the new, larger ships that were constructed in the shipyard, the Minnesota River was dredged for 14 miles to a minimum depth of 9 feet. Once the ships left Savage, they sailed down the Mississippi River to New Orleans, where they were fitted with their final equipment. One of them, the USS *Namakagon* was launched in November 1944.

Clara arranged a ride to the Norfolk shipyard, and she hastily kissed Glenn good-bye. She boarded a bus to return to North Dakota, and he arrived in New Orleans on the 13th. He boarded the USS *Namakagon* on the day after its commissioning.

Glenn wrote in a letter to Clara, dated June 15, 1945,

> "Well, Darling, here I sit with a 12 to 4 AM watch, so I might as well whip out a letter. I suppose you are on your merry way home by now…I wish I was going along with you, to tell the truth…Yesterday they put me in charge of a working party, so you see, I'm getting my prestige back. Tonight I am P.O. (Petty Officer) of the watch, all I do is sit here behind a big desk and fill out the log, but this is a hell of a time to be up.

My trusty tanker looks to be a pretty good outfit. She's small and fast and has a lot of maneuverability. Electricians have to stand throttle watches. So that will be something new for me. There is no Chief Electrician, just another first class, so I imagine yours truly will get plenty of headaches... This guy on watch with me here is trying to tell me his life's history, guess I'll have to shoot him to shut him up."

Gee honey, it would have been nice if I could have stayed here a couple of months so you could have come down...Just think, I won't be able to continue giving you swimming instructions...I'd like to see you tonight rolling along on that bus...it looks to me like you should get home about Sunday.

Everything is sticky down here from this damp heat...The cock roaches are playing a game of baseball on my desk here. The place is busy with bugs.

This is kind of a bad time for you to be traveling around the country, too... I hope you write a letter on the way, so I'll know how you're getting along. Bye Darling, I love you, XXXX Glenn XXX."

The tanker sailed into Mobile, Alabama, on June 24, and Glenn met with his brother-in-law, Dick Jordan, for a short visit. They had a lot to talk about, including their wives, the Schweigert sisters. On July 4, the tanker was at Galveston, Texas, and after completing her Gulf coast shakedown, they filled gasoline at Baytown, Texas, and departed for the Pacific via the Panama Canal. The war against Japan in the Pacific continued to rage on. President Truman's advisors warned him that any attempt to invade Japan would result in horrific American casualties. By August 1945, the Allies "Manhattan Project" had produced two types of atomic bombs. Truman ordered that the new weapon be used to bring a speedy end to the war and save American lives.

On August 6, a Boeing B-29 *Superfortress*, *Enola Gay*, dropped "Little Boy," a five-ton devastating uranium bomb over Hiroshima. It immediately killed 80,000 people, but Japan did not surrender to the Allies.

The next day, August 7, the *Namakagon* pulled into San Diego, California. To Glenn's disappointment, he discovered that Clara was not back in Coronado yet. She had stayed on her parents' farm near Stanton, North Dakota, too long.

On August 9, Glenn wrote,

"I suppose by now you are getting pretty close to California. It was sure too bad the way things worked out for us, but now with Russia in the war and this new bomb we have, maybe it won't be long until we are back together for good...

I don't guess you got to see Duane. I still can't get over the fact that he got out of the Army. He sure didn't waste any time getting an airplane, did he? Dad is just like a little kid where Duane and his plane are concerned...

I got seven letters from you one day and three the next... If it weren't for those letters, a guy would get pretty lonesome."

As the tanker sailed for Pearl Harbor, on August 9, the United States dropped another devastating bomb, this time on the city of Nagasaki, Japan. This one, a plutonium implosive bomb, had the code name of "Fat Man." Roughly half of the deaths in each city occurred on the first day. Still, Japan did not surrender to the Allies immediately.

Glenn's letter to Clara on August 12 said,

"I guess the war is about to wind itself up for good. It doesn't hardly seem possible after being in it so long, but I will have something to look forward to now anyway. If it actually does end now, I wonder how l long it will take me to get out. Quite a while, I suppose. There seem to be a few million other guys just as anxious as me to get out...I suppose harvest is going in full swing at home now. Oh, well, I'll bet you I don't miss another one. I wonder if Duane will help the folks out this year...Did you go back to work at Safeway (grocery store)?...I'll bet there will really

be some celebrations in the states when they proclaim Victory in Japan Day...When I get back, we can both go out and celebrate.

If you ever run into a good car (if there is any) out there, that's not too high priced, go ahead and buy it, and we will drive back home someday. I trust you are a good judge of automobiles? That would be a nice trip if we had a car and just took our time. Post-war planning. I wouldn't care much what it looks like, just so it would run that far.

Maybe next time I write, we will be at peace, I hope. I love you and always will darling. Oh, yes, I heard from DeMarco, and it was pretty old by the time I got it. He tried to find me in Norfolk when he got there but, of course, I was gone. He said he heard from someone on the ship, and they said our Presidential Citation had gone through, so I suppose I will be hearing about it one of these days."

Japan Surrenders August 14
"Today has been one of the happiest days of my life."

"Pulled into Pearl Harbor on August 14, 1945, The Japanese surrendered unconditionally, and the war is over at last. HOORAY! My Darling Wife, Today has been about one of the happiest days of my life. I really can look forward to getting back to you before too long now. It seems funny to think that the war is actually over. I guess it will take me a while to realize it.

You know, when I first came into the Navy, about all I thought about was home and the farm and about the folks, and things like that. Since we met and married, everything seems to center around you. I don't know whether you will be happy back home on the farm or not, but I believe that two persons who love each other can make out most any place."

Glenn started standing watch again while at Pearl Harbor, and also connected with his Navy brother-in-law. *"I saw Dick today twice, so we had a nice long visit. It doesn't look like he will be going back to the states for a while either. It looks like you two will be old maids for some time yet...I may run into Fritz* (Clara's brother, Fred Schweigert) *sometime, too."*

"Arrived at Midway on August 23. It is just a small sandpile with an airstrip and harbor." Glenn reported that he went ashore the next day, had a couple of beers and saw Gooney bird airplanes for the first time. These transport aircraft were developed from the civilian Douglas DC-3 airliner and were used extensively during WW II by the Allies. The ship left Midway and headed for Saipan, crossing the International Date Line, where they lost 24 hours.

When the other First Class Electrician became ill, Glenn had his hands full standing watch and being in charge of the EM2s and 3s. He requested Clara to send him a camera and some film so he could take some pictures now that the war was over. Prior to this, they were not allowed to do so, and their letters were censored.

CHAPTER 23

Saipan and Japan

GLENN'S WORLD WAR II JOURNEY CONTINUED in the Asiatic-Pacific.

"Arrived at Saipan on September 2, 1945. The harbor is full of small craft, with over 500 ships in all." The next day, Glenn wrote, "I got ten letters from you today and I'm so happy after reading them, that I don't know whether to laugh or cry. There is nothing that can make me so happy as knowing I have such a sweet, loving wife waiting for me.

Raymond and Lillie using a Model-B Ford for harvesting, 1945

Well, I guess they finally signed the peace treaty, so now I can tell you just where I am. We left right from Diego for Pearl Harbor, where I saw Dick. We pulled into Midway and got cargo and, we left the next day for Saipan. Today about noon, we anchored here in Saipan.

I had a nice long letter from Fritz (Clara's brother) today. He also gave me instructions on how to find him in Manila. We may go there from here...I heard from the folks, too. They have been combining some (wheat), but it isn't running too good, 12 or 13 to the acre, I guess. Duane is going to help them until harvest is over, and then he and Martin are going to start their flying school. Duane has his plane and one of Martin's down at Regent now. I guess he has been flying quite a bit. His plane is an Army trainer."

Dad says he hopes to hell I get home pretty quick so I can take the farm over...

Glenn continued to write to Clara about his friend,

'So old Amos and Phyllis (Tollefson) got married. Mom said they had quite a wedding.

Sweetheart, I think those six weeks we spent together were great, but I think the next sixty years will be better...All my love and bushels of kisses.

Your loving sailor-farmer, Glenn"

The *Namakagon* took on a load of fuel oil from a large tanker to fill small craft in Saipan. Glenn fixed a whaleboat generator that wasn't charging, and reported,

"There are a bunch of Japanese ships and also ours sunk around here. You can see parts of them sticking up out of the water...We pulled out

amongst the other ships today and anchored, we have a full load on now. We aren't going to move for a while now, so we started pulling our main generators apart to clean up and paint."

I made a little oven today to bake the varnish on armatures and stuff, pretty neat little gadget if I do say so myself. I have been working my boys pretty hard the last couple of days; we have a lot of work to catch up on now that we aren't underway. When we are at sea, it's pretty hard to get much done. They aren't crazy about working very hard, but I don't have much trouble. There is one second-class that is really a screwball though. Everything he touches he fouls up. I stand watch with him, too.

It doesn't hardly seem possible that we will be together forever pretty soon, does it? And nothing can tear us apart again. To hell with the grasshoppers and the dust storms and the drought, as long as we are together. Well, darling, it's time to go to the movie. We are having a good one tonight, 'Tall in the Saddle' with John Wayne. Oh boy, my favorite cowboy!!

I love you and always will, Glenn"

A couple days later they took on some aviation gasoline in preparation for departure for Okinawa and then Japan. Glenn reported, *"I did a little work yesterday...I tore a generator down and cleaned it and varnished the field coils and put it back together again by myself in half a day, just to show the guys how fast it could be done. Some of them piddled around a whole day. It is too hot here to even sleep. I am now out on the rail enjoying a cool rain."*

Glenn's morale sank over the discharge point system, and he reported:

"Here I am with 43 points, and the rest of the men with enough points will be leaving in a couple of days. And I have to stay on for the sake of one stinking point. It will take at least a month and a half at this present system before I will make 44 and, then Lord only knows, where we will be and whether they will let me go or not. We are going to have to pick up some replacements pretty soon, or we will be shorthanded.

It looks to me like they would send some of these small ships back to the states. They sure aren't doing any good out here. There are 300 or 400 anchored right here that could just as well go back and be decommissioned. The sailors out here haven't got much chance of getting out as long as all these ships have to be manned.

I haven't set foot ashore since we were in Midway over three weeks ago, and then we just walked over on the Island (of Saipan) for an hour or so."

The next day, September 15, Glenn stood watch and then:

"this afternoon I fooled around making an ashtray out of some brass shell casings."

Side shells are 20mm MK4-1944. Center, 50-caliber 3" MK7 shell

Okinawa, Japan

The next stop was Okinawa on September 21. The next day Glenn reported:

"We got in here yesterday and are leaving again about noon today. The rumor is that we are shoving off for Nagasaki, wherever that is, but I can't be sure yet. We are heading for Japan. This place has a great big bay and it's jammed full of ships of all kinds. There are a couple of big flattops and seven or eight wagons and a whole bunch of smaller fighting craft. I guess we are going to take our load of gasoline with us to Japan...I sure am getting a long way from home now, roughly 8,000 miles from the states. You are walking right on top of me in case you don't know it."

Sasebo, Japan

"Arrived at Sasebo Naval Base, Sasebo, Japan, on September 25. We anchored out off the beach a couple of hundred yards...This is sure a pretty spot. We came into a narrow channel and could see the Japanese on the beach there, and then into a nice quiet harbor here. There are big mountains all around us. The Japanese have them terraced and are raising stuff on the slopes." Occasionally, a dead body would float past the ship. *"They said this place had been only taken a couple of days now."*

Glenn was eager to go into the city with a liberty party and check it over.

"They go over in groups and walk around town, they can't go into any Japanese dwelling or fool around with anything. Only one electrician can go at a time...I finally got ashore yesterday...We had to stay in a group, and we walked all over. It was all bombed to hell in the middle of town. We walked block after block in different places where it was all leveled right down to the ground. You see a few chimneys and stuff sticking up out of the rubble. I can see now just why these people surrendered.

The Japanese are all little (people), you can hardly tell the difference between the kids and the adults. The kids and women are pretty friendly, but the men haven't much use for us. The kids have already learned a few American words; they ask for cigarettes and gum. I traded cigarettes for the money and the picture to kids. I guess the picture is the boy's mother or sister. You can take that picture and money and hang onto it for me.

All the boys and men wear uniforms, while the women wear these funny looking slack outfits, and I do mean slack. You run into some funny-looking individuals. A lot of them wear these thick-lensed glasses and have big buck teeth. What impressed me most is the fact that they are so darn small.

I got a ride back to the ship in a big motor launch from another ship. It was a real rough sea, and our (ship's) own whaleboat went under coming back, but they saved the men in it and got them aboard another ship for the night. So I was lucky I wasn't in it. I just missed it by a few minutes."

On October 3, Glenn received a Facsimile, or exact copy of his "Presidential Unit Citation Award to the Anti-submarine Task Group 22.3, 4 June 1944, from the Chief of Naval Personnel. He also received a ribbon bar with bronze star" for being a member of Boarding Party #3 USS *Guadalcanal*, but there was no one from the Task Force that captured the submarine to celebrate with him.

A few days later on October 6 Glenn wrote:

"What do you know, I saw Dick Jordan (brother-in-law) again today. His ship (USS Fallon, *an attack transport, was one of the first ships to occupy Japan) pulled in here this morning with a load of troops, so this afternoon I bummed a ride over there in the boat and visited him. I was surprised the Division Officer would let me go over there today when I asked him, but he never even gave me a growl. He sure is an ornery old devil. Yesterday, we had a motor that was sparking badly on the boiler for the last month or so, and I kept telling him we should secure it and fix it. But he says, 'No, let it go as long as it runs,' so I did, and sure enough it*

burned up last night. So we just took our sweet time fixing it. That little deal probably cost the Navy 100 bucks or so.

I heard yesterday that the ship got an order that they couldn't hold men after they got their 44 points. I hope it is true, because I will have 44 the 1st of November, the Yeoman tells me. So maybe I will be getting out in Nov. and back to the states around the first of Dec. That would be just right for us to take a couple of weeks going home before Christmas."

A typhoon blew in while they were anchored at Saipan in October. Glenn noted that Dick's ship, the trusty old 81 (USS *Fallon*) was about a 100 yards away from them and waiting out the storm in the harbor before starting for the Philippines.

"We are right in the midst of a typhoon here now. It started this morning... It has been too rough for any small boats in the water today, so we didn't get any movies or see about the mail. Some of these smaller ships are dragging their anchors all over the harbor.

We finally sent off the men with over 44 points. They left yesterday morning for a transport back to the states. Two electricians got off, the other first class and a second class, so that leaves us with only five men. We might get a striker or two from the deck division now. Anyway, it leaves me first in line for a transfer now. It's getting closer and closer now. I also seem to be senior man in the whole engineering outfit now.

There are going to be a couple of boxing matches tonight, but I guess I'll miss them, as I think I have the 8 to 12 (watch). As long as the storm keeps up, we have to keep a throttle watch on so we can get underway if we have to.... Boy, I wish I was going back to the states now, I'm getting sick of these foreign ports and homesick for the good old U.S.A. and, naturally, I miss my wife."

The next day, Glenn wrote that he heard over the radio that Okinawa caught hell from the typhoon. Winds of 130 mph leveled the barracks and everything, and 90 tons of mail was lost in the storm. Four days later, he was thrilled to receive six letters from Clara, which made his world look pretty rosy again. *"A couple of the letters had been wet, so I have an idea they were fished out of the drink in Okinawa."*

He continued:

"You bet your sweet life we are going to have a white Christmas this year.

It will be my first in three years, and I suppose about the same for you. Won't that be wonderful, though, to know we will be together for always…If we could get a car cheap and drive home, but I am afraid they are still pretty high priced. I don't guess the weather would bother us much, hardy Pioneers that we are."

There isn't much a guy can do over here. Another guy and I rented a ride around in a rickshaw, a big time! The ship put in for some souvenirs for the crew the other day. So today they went over to the beach to get them. They came back with 12 Jap rifles and a bunch of dishes and crap like that, and I'll be dammed if the officers didn't take all the rifles for themselves. Everybody was so mad about the deal that none would take any of the rest of the stuff.

I just got through running a shoot-em-up western picture, 'The Yellow Rose of Texas' was the name of it with Roy Rogers. I believe these guys enjoy a picture like that, as well as any. I have run 10 pictures so far this month so that means 10 bucks, pretty easy money.

Tomorrow we are going to secure the gyrocompass and clean and oil it, so that should take up the biggest part of the day. I haven't had a haircut since I had it cut off short, so I look like a violin player or something."

He was also dreaming about his wife.

Clara was an animal lover

"My Dearest Darling, You were in my dreams last night...I could see you just as plain as could be, you were holding a cat in your arms too. I don't know how that cat got in our dreams, but it did. Anyway, it was kind of funny because I could see you standing there holding that dam yellow cat all day."

"The boss stopped me this morning and said he thought he had some good news for me, but wasn't sure yet. He said they had heard that they could get me a replacement here on the beach, and that he would let me know as soon as he found out...We might take a train into Salt Lake City and see how used cars are selling there, and we could also see how the weather situation looked from there. Of course, I don't know where I will land in the states. It could be L.A. or Frisco or Seattle."

He continued, *"I had a nice long letter from your dad today, but no others. It always sort of surprises me, after reading the stern letters 'Office of County Judge' to see such a friendly letter."* (Clara's father, C.F. Schweigert, was Mercer County Judge at Stanton, North Dakota, from 1931 to 1961.)

The end of October, Glenn was daydreaming about North Dakota. *"I sure wish I could get back for the deer season this year, it is the 26-30 of November, but I see that I could never make that unless I grow wings."*

Then came the long awaited announcement.

"The boss called me up to his room this noon and, as soon as I stepped in the door, he asked me how long it would take me to pack. I was afraid he was kidding, but he said they had decided to release me as soon as they could get transportation back to the States after the 3rd (Nov)....Boy I could have taken off and flown home after I heard that. I hope I have a little luck in getting a fairly fast ship back now...Maybe I'll be back by the first of December yet.

I hope this news makes you as happy as it makes me, darling...A first class machinist is going at the same time I do. He's running around here like a crazy Indian. I asked him why he didn't go to bed and he says, 'Oh hell, I couldn't sleep anyway, so I guess he feels about like me tonight...Sit tight now baby, and I shall battle my way back across the vast expanses of the Pacific Ocean and deliver myself at my loved one's doorstep."

"November 3, 1945, Sasebo, Japan, I am all packed and ready to go this evening...I have been having quite a time figuring out what to take with me and what to leave behind. The big bag weighs about a ton now, more or less.

This morning, we had inspection and this afternoon, I worked rigging up an electric motor to put on the ice cream freezer. I was kind of surprised at how slick it worked. We had payday today, too, but I left mine on the books because I already have over 100 in cash on me. I might get lifted before I get back.

I got your letter yesterday with the picture of yourself, and I just say I didn't do bad at all at choosing a wife...I liked the picture a lot. I often wonder just how a big sap like me ever got a person like you for a wife...It sure gets chilly here at night now. I guess winter must be coming. What I need is someone to keep me warm."

The next day, Glenn reported:

"I am leaving the ship in the morning and going over to the Port Director for transportation. So I will be discharged at Terminal Island or Pedro (California), they are both the same. But you might as well stay in San Diego until you hear from me. It will probably be a month or so before I get there, if I am lucky.

I am on my way at last, and I can hardly wait to get there. I love you, sweetheart, and it won't be long now."

CHAPTER 24

Homeward Bound
Ships, Trains, Planes and Automobiles

AFTER THREE LONG YEARS OF SERVING his country, Glenn was finally going home. He grunted under the weight of his overstuffed seabag that he carried onto the USS *Dauphin*. He left Sasebo, Japan, on November 6, 1945, aboard an attack transport carrying eager troops bound for California.

In the meantime, Aunt Carrie Noben wrote to Clara:

> *"How are you getting along? And is Glenn coming soon? Hope you two*
> *can come and see us before you go back to North Dakota. I had a letter*
> *from Lillie today, and all is well, but they are getting anxious for you and*
> *Glenn to come home...Duane is at home now. I think he goes between*
> *Regent and Martin's place. Did you know Martin has bought the ranch*
> *where he is living? (near Fort Clark, North Dakota). Well, dear, I just*
> *wanted you to know we think of you often and hope we will see you and*
> *Glenn soon.*
>
> *Lots of love, Aunt Carrie."*

It took the *Dauphin* 19 days to transit the Pacific Ocean, which seemed forever for Glenn. Finally, he laid his eyes on the bustling port city ahead. Boats and ships of all sizes and kinds, ferries and tugs towing barges. He was back in the United States and safe. He was Honorably Discharged from the U.S. Navy Personnel Separation Center at San Pedro, California, on the 25th day of November 1945.

Now all he could think about was a joyful reunion with his beloved wife. With great anticipation, Glenn rode a bus, a street car, and then a ferry to

Coronado Island, ending up at Helene and Dick's house. What ecstasy to finally be back together with Clara.

War has a strange and compelling way of changing people, including Glenn. It is the worst thing in the world. It causes both fear and excitement; an adrenaline rush, and it may inflict both physical and emotional injuries. A sense of meaning and purpose grows out of working together, protecting and being protected by their comrades, giving them a shared commitment and brotherhood. It is a warrior's fight between good and evil, and it accentuates one's own mortality. *The heart of a man is like deep water...*Proverbs 20:5.

With his battle and adventure over, Glenn retrieved his beauty and began searching for an automobile. Fortunately, Clara had saved $500 while working at Safeway Food Store's meat department. Due to rationing during WWII, no new cars had been produced from 1942 to 1945, and vehicles were in short supply now.

After doing some searching, Glenn located a rusty car that he felt he could afford and that would get them home. He purchased the car and promptly drove it to Helene and Dick's home. Here he parked it on the lawn and prepared it for painting. After a quick trip to a hardware store, he painted it black using spray cans. Clara recalled that it looked much better after it was painted, at least from a distance. It would look satisfactory for their triumphal return entry into Regent, North Dakota. To test-drive the car, they ventured north to San Francisco for a short visit with his brother, Wayne, wife Flo, and little daughter, Bonnie.

While Clara and Helene's husbands were away at sea , the sisters had been busy canning ripe fruits and vegetables that Clara brought home from the grocery store. Now these jars were carefully packed into the newlyweds' car, along with their luggage. Clara, always an animal lover, had agreed to take Helene's little dog, Rags, back to North Dakota. Helene and Dick were moving and unable to keep her. So Rags was also loaded into their car before departure. Hoping to avoid the northern Rocky Mountain snow, Glenn headed east, excited to be on the open road, heading toward home at last.

By the time they reached Las Vegas, he was unable to shift the gears in his little black gem. Even with a faulty transmission, he was able to strike up a deal for the junker with "Mad Man Pizzinger," a used car salesman.

He received half the payment for the car immediately and Mr. Pizzinger promised him the other half when he received the title in the mail, which was on its way to Regent.

The undaunted couple found a hotel and checked into it until they could figure out what to do next. One dilemma was what to do with Clara's little dog. After brainstorming, Glenn built a small crate and had her shipped by train to Regent.

Clara now gave up on getting her glass jars of home-canned produce home with her, and gifted them to the lady who managed the hotel. Next they purchased bus tickets to Salt Lake City. Upon arrival, they discovered a bus and train strike going on. Now what would they do?

After some research, Glenn discovered he could purchase plane tickets to Helena, Montana, but he was skeptical about the safety of flying commercial, since the airline business was so new in 1945. To him, the early airliners resembled flying box cars. However, with limited options, they purchased tickets on a packed airplane, boarded with trepidation and excitement, and made a new memory.

The plane landed safely at Helena, getting them closer to North Dakota.

Back home, Glenn found a 1937 Chevrolet coupe.

CHAPTER 25

Home for a White Christmas

WHAT A RELIEF TO FIND THAT trains were operating in Montana. They transferred their luggage and boarded the Northern Pacific for their last train ride into Dickinson, North Dakota. Bursting with excitement, Raymond and Lillie welcomed them at the depot. Overcome with feelings of joy, relief, and thankfulness, they shared warm hugs and tears of joy. Lillie reported to them that Clara's little dog, Rags, had arrived safely at Regent.

With the luggage loaded, Raymond and his passengers headed south for the last 50 miles of their journey. He drove past the little town of New England, and then turned east toward Regent and their farm. During this exciting time, conversation flowed. It was good to be safe and home again with family at last.

When Glenn and Clara arrived at Regent in December, they only had 100 dollars left between them. But Glenn, however, had his final Navy pay coming in the mail, and also the remaining car payment from Mad Man Pizzinger.

The weather turned cold, but love warmed their hearts. Two days later, they attended the Christmas Eve program at the little town's Congregational Church. They were greeted by old friends, sang Christmas hymns, and watched the children portray Jesus' birth. What a glorious gift of salvation God gave to the world that first night in Bethlehem.

Glenn and Clara relished the white Christmas for which they had been longing, and being together with their family. Winter turned into spring, and Glenn returned to farming the land where he had grown to manhood. Nearby baby calves frolicked, as their mothers grazed on new prairie grass and wild onion plants near the creek that meandered to the Cannonball River. Spring wheat and corn emerged verdant and vigorous in the freshly planted fields. That summer, as Glenn cultivated the corn fields, he again daydreamed about how he had sailed the high seas and helped win the biggest and deadliest war in history. Yes, life was hard, but God is Good.

Glenn and Clara eventually took over the family farm and raised six children, along with small grains, cattle, sheep, and horses. Glenn and Clara operated a dairy farm at Regent, and he delivered fresh milk to the folks in the little village in the early years. Clara assisted him with bottling the milk and washing the bottles.

Glenn's young neighbor, Kasper Binstock, sometimes helped with the milk delivery and recalled that when the snow was too deep to drive a vehicle, they used a team of horses.

After the war, Mildred Bowers Smith and her husband, Jim, lived with their children in Regent where he worked at the Regent Garage. With help from Leonard Prince, Jim purchased a PT-13 surplus training aircraft and enjoyed giving thrill rides to volunteers. It had a powerful engine, two seats and a glass dome. One day Glenn went along for a ride, and while Jim was flying the plane upside down, Glenn's seat suddenly broke loose. The unnerving incident became another humorous adventure for Glenn to recall and have fun sharing.

After WW II, Glenn's brother, Duane, managed Wyman's Airport at Mott, North Dakota. He was assisted by his pilot cousin, Geneva Schow, who was born three miles east of Regent in 1924 at her grandparent's farm. She grew up at Stanton, North Dakota, where she was thrilled to ride in the open cockpit airplane owned by her father, Martin. Geneva earned her private pilot's license at Dickinson, North Dakota, in 1945. While assisting with managing the Mott Airport, she created *Dakota Flyer* in November 1946, the

Geneva Schow

Martin Schow and the biplane he and Johnny Osterhouse built in 1927

first aviation publication in North Dakota. It covered news about aviation training, flyers, airports and organizations such as Flying Farmers and the Civil Air Patrol.

Geneva married Todd Oleson on July 9, 1948, and continued her publication, until she turned it over to Carl T. Thompson in 1949. Her untiring efforts to advance all stages of early aviation in North Dakota led to her induction into the North Dakota Aviation Hall of Fame in 2013. She was the first woman to receive this aviation honor in North Dakota.

Geneva's father, Martin Schow, and his good friend, Johnny Osterhouse, of Regent, built an airplane in 1927 at Stanton, North Dakota, using parts from a busted up Travel Air plane. Martin's wife, Madeline, the daughter of George and Laura (Switzer) Tooker of Regent, sewed Indian Head linen to cover the wings and interior. A sealing nitrate dope was applied to the fabric.

Martin learned to fly by first taxiing around to get the feel for the plane and its controls. He would test the lift slightly and then settle the plane back down on the ground. Finally, after hours of practice in a field near Stanton, he became airborne for his first short flight, as Madeline took photographs to document the event. With his new wings, Martin would no longer feel helpless in an emergency situation like the one that took the lives of his first wife, Olga Anderson, of Regent, and their unborn baby when they homesteaded near Roundup, Montana. That fall in 1927, Martin flew to Fargo to attend the Lindbergh Day Banquet where he met and was inspired by Charles Lindbergh, the featured speaker. Martin Schow was inducted into the North Dakota Aviation Hall of Fame in 2014.

Legendary Johnny Osterhouse

Martin taught his friend, Johnny Osterhouse to fly. Osterhouse took over the management of the Ben Eielson Air Field on the strip at Mandan, North Dakota in 1929. He transformed it from a field into Mandan's first airport, which he managed for five years. He opened a flying school, provided charter flights, gave rides to hundreds of people (including Gov. Bill Langer), and initiated night flying in the Bismarck-Mandan area.

Osterhouse also flew to Regent to teach area residents to fly and formed the Regent Areo Club around 1929. Some members were James Marks, Sammy Lane, Raymond and Russell Larson, Johnny Jungers, and Adam Zollner, the town barber. September 27, 1929, was an exciting day when two local men decided to jump out of a perfectly good airplane, according to the *Regent Times*:

> "A large crowd estimated at 4,000 gathered at the Regent flying field last Sunday afternoon, when over 800 cars formed a circle around the field to witness the parachute jumping scheduled for that day. The crowd received a big thrill when at 2 p.m. "Lucky" Ernest Hagenston, at an altitude of 2,000 feet, stepped from the wing of a plane piloted by Ed Canfield of Williston. He made a successful descent and landed easily on his feet without mishap.
>
> At 5:30, John Osterhouse repeated the stunt from the Canfield plane. His parachute opened gracefully, and he, too, made a safe and easy landing."

In 1930, when Glenn was eight years old, his uncle, Martin Schow, and Osterhouse started putting on air shows around the region. At the airshow in Glasgow, Montana, Osterhouse tied with Tex Rankin of Portland, Oregon, the current world champion, in doing 22 arial loops in five minutes.

One day Osterhouse pulled off a daring event. Witnesses watched as he flew his plane solo upside down under the Bismarck/Mandan Memorial Bridge.

Legendary Johnny Osterhouse

Another outstanding feat occurred in 1935 when Osterhouse landed his plane at the Mandan Airport with a broken landing gear. It happened as he took off from a field at Golden Valley, North Dakota, during the annual Mercer County Old Settlers' picnic. After Osterhouse noticed the broken gear and informed his six passengers, he flew back over the Golden Valley Airport where he dropped a note tied to a wrench, instructing attendants to call Mandan Airport to have an ambulance and a fire truck waiting for them at the airport.

While Johnny circled the Mandan Airport, his courageous student, J.D. Wilson, crept out on the wing, caught the landing gear with safety belts, and held it in place during the landing. Skillfully, Osterhouse managed a two-point landing. As the plane skidded on the ground, it tilted slightly on one wing and did a half ground loop, landing in a cloud of dust. The tense drama ended in the safe landing of six men and a 3-year old boy, Reuben C. Unruh of Zap, North Dakota.

On August 21, 1935, Osterhouse married his high school sweetheart, Mildred Lane, who was teaching at Sharon, North Dakota. She was the daughter of Lansford and Rosa (Leavitt) Lane of Regent. Her father worked in Regent's First State Bank.

The newlyweds lived in Mott, where Mildred became the Hettinger County Superintendent of Schools. Times were tough during the Dirty 30s, so in November 1935 Johny accepted a stunt flying job with the Hell Divers Air Circus out of Corpus Christi, Texas. He became known as "Upside Down Johnny Osterhouse" because he flew inverted and low over the crowd at the beginning of the shows.

The Hell Divers held a Regent airshow that included wing walking, the act of moving on the wing of an airplane during flight. Harold Bach recalled that they landed at the Regent airstrip behind the schoolhouse. The show included Osterhouse and also Lina Basquet, a beautiful French girl in a flowing dress who did parachute jumps and the dangerous wing walking.

Lina Schow Lamsters of Stanton, North Dakota, reminisced that Lina Basquet was a professional ballerina and silent movie star. She married her first husband, Sam Warner, of the Warner brothers film studio in 1925. He was much older than her, and unfortunatley, died two years later. The Warner family took custody of their daughter, Lita, and Lina was unofficially blacklisted in Hollywood. She fell on hard times and apparently took the wing walking job with the Hell Divers Air Circus before returning to sound films.

Glenn remembered that members of the Flying Circus visited their farm by Larson Lake when he was a boy. He was intrigued by the monkey they brought with them, which perched on top of a door while Lillie served lunch.

John and Mildred Osterhouse's son, Jack, was born on July 8, 1936. In November, four months later, while home in Regent to visit family, area farmers requested Johnny and his co-pilot, Archie Geiser, hunt coyotes, because the animals were aggressively killing sheep. With Archie flying the plane, Johnny, the gunner, sat in the front seat of the open cockpit bi-plane for a wide view as they circled Black Butte.

The cause of the November 15 crash is a mystery. Tragically, the plane nosed into the ground from an altitude of about 50 feet. Dr. Hill, Ed Colgrove, and Gordon Stewart were hunting in the vicinity and arrived shortly after the crash. Dr. Hill, however, was unable to save Johnny's life and he died just a few miles from where he was born and raised. His friend, Archie Giesser, sustained a broken ankle and fractured jaw.

Glenn, age 13, and the entire community were shocked by Johnny's death. Harold Bach, a teenager, was in the Regent Garage when the news broke and he recalled the great grief among the men. Tears flowed down Glenn's Uncle Russell Larson's cheeks. Russell drove the gas truck for the Farmer's Union Oil Company and was not only one of Johnny's students, but one of his many friends.

The love for Johnny was evident by the hundreds of friends and fellow aviators from seven states that attended his funeral. It was moved from Regent's Congregational Church to Woodman's Hall to accommodate the large crowd. The mourners proceeded to the Regent Cemetery, where aviators dropped flowers and wreaths onto and near Osterhouse's casket from the air in their last salute to their beloved friend.

Osterhouse's wife moved to Washington to be with family and remarried in 1940. Devastated by the loss of his dear friend, Martin Show commissioned an artist to paint a life-sized oil portrait of Johnny Osterhouse. Years later, the Schow family gifted the painting to Johnny's son, Jack Rodstrom, of Prescott, Arizona.

When Osterhouse' son, Jack and wife, Olga, visited Regent several years ago on their motorcycle, Glenn's friend and local resident, Dale Stewart,

Esther Sundby and Duane Larson's wedding day

Glenn and his new wings, a J-3 Cub

showed them great hospitality. Jack reported that he has photo and newspaper albums from his father, mother, and Johnny's friend, Archie Giesser.

Glenn's brothers

While managing the airport at Mott after World War II, Glenn's brother, Duane, started a GI flying school, called The Dakota Flyers. Over the next four years he instructed over 150 students, flew charter flights and introduced aerial crop spraying to western North Dakota. He married Esther Sundby of Turtle Lake in 1947 when they eloped in his airplane to Wibaux, Montana. They were the parents of four children, Linda Engelman, Thomas, Steve and James Peter.

Duane spent six years in the Air Force Reserve and then joined the North Dakota Air National Guard's 178th Fighter Interceptor Squadron of the 119th Fighter Group in 1951. The unit was dubbed "The Happy Hooligans" and as their commanding officer, Duane became known as "Pappy." He retired from the ND Guard in 1969 as Brigadier General and then flew crop-dusting planes for eight years. He accrued more than 10,000 flight hours during his flying career and was inducted into the North Dakota Aviation Hall of Fame as a charter member in 1997. Duane's son, Thomas, followed in his footsteps and became a F-16 pilot with the North Dakota Air National Guard. Duane died at the age of 88 in 2005, and is buried at the North Dakota Veteran's Cemetery south of Mandan.

Duane taught close to 200 students to fly, including Glenn. After Glenn earned his private pilot's license, he purchased his own airplane. In 1947, when his second son, Roger, was born, he flew Clara and baby home from Dickinson, and landed in the pasture north of the farmyard.

Glenn's brother, Wayne, stayed in San Francisco after he was discharged from the Army in October 1945. He worked for the Pacific Telephone and Telegraph Company in the toll division, which handled long distance circuits, radio and television broadcasting. Ten year later he advanced to the engineering end, and retired in 1981, with more time to enjoy his family and hobby as a Ham Radio operator. Wayne and Flo were parents of four children, Bonita Culdice, Russell, Janet and Steve. Wayne died at age 91 in 2009.

Never one to sit still, Glenn helped organize Regent's Sod Buster's Saddle Club after the war. They usually met on Sunday afternoons at Larson Lake until an arena was built in Regent. One fall, he and his friend, Kelly Rutherford, drove to a special horse sale in Miles City, Montana, where he purchased a registrable foundation Quarter Horse filly and named her Ginger. Glenn spent many hours training her and she became not only his favorite horse, but also the family's.

In the 1950s Glenn hired a young man, Lee Soehren, from Regent to help him with his chores. Lee recalled:

"I was really excited to go to work for your dad. Great guy, I really enjoyed working for him. He and Alton Ivy were good friends and Alton was a cousin of mine ....I really didn't know Glenn, but when he asked

me to work for him and that I would have a horse to ride, the deal was
made. I started with Alton Ivey's pony, Queenie. She was in her 20s and
very kid friendly. She put up with me and taught me how to be a cowboy.
Eventually Glenn said, 'Lee, it's time to start using my horse (Ginger).'

She was half thoroughbred, young, and Glenn had trained her himself.
Lee continued:

"Wow, was I excited, or what? I had to learn how to bridle and saddle
a real cowboy horse. I could run and leapfrog onto Queenie, but that
was not going to happen with Ginger. I could hardly get my leg up high
enough to put my foot in the stirrup. Ginger was a very patient horse and
a half-sister to Gene Autry's horse, Champion. Now I was a real cowboy.
She was well trained and even responded going right or left by shifting
your weight in the saddle."

Lee reminisced about another way that Glenn mentored him.

"It was one of those days when it rained all day. Your dad said, 'Let's
paint your car, Lee.' My car was a 1939 Chevy, faded blue, but otherwise
great. He found a can of maroon paint, my favorite color. You know the
old maroon and gold of the Regent Rangers. So we did it. We had to prep
it for painting and we did it in one of his sheds. It turned out great. Every
kid in Hettinger County knew and many parents knew it was me (in that
car). I didn't go around spinning the tires like the kids with bigger cars. I
drove it all through high school and into college."

One winter Glenn put his mechanical skills to work by taking a job at
Luke Jungers' garage. Glenn also assisted in the formation of the Regent
Airport Authority in 1961, and the Regent Flying Club in 1966. The club then
purchased a Piper J-3 Cub for member use.

In 1963, Glenn and Clara purchased the Hettinger Livestock Sales Barn
at Hettinger, North Dakota, in partnership with Lawrence and Rose Strand
of Regent.

Glenn in 1960   *Clara and Glenn in 1970s*

They returned to dairy farming intermittently, including a few years at Eagle Bend, Minnesota.

In 1972 they moved to Ellendale, North Dakota, where they owned and operated the Oxenrider Motel, and farmed for several years. Their final move was to a ranch north of McClusky in 1980, to be near their daughter, Bev, husband Steve, and three grandsons.

Both of Glenn and Clara's sons followed in their father's footsteps and enlisted in the US Navy. James joined the Navy in 1965 and after basic training, he trained at Electrician Mate School in San Diego, Nuclear Power School at Vallejo, California, and at the Atomic Energy Arco Test Site, Arco, Idaho. Upon completion, Jim attended Submarine School in Gronton, Connecticut, and went on to serve as an Electrician's Mate 1st Class onboard the nuclear attack submarine, the USS *Grayling*, from 1967 to 1971.

Roger earned his private pilot's license while attending college at Dickinson, North Dakota, and joined the Navy in 1970. After training and carrier landing qualifications, he became a flight instructor for the carrier-based fighter aircraft, the Grumman F-9/F-9F Cougar at Pensacola. Next he did flight instruction on the A-4 Skyhawk attack aircraft at Pensacola and

Glenn and Clara's family in 1983
Back left to right: Dorothy, Shirley, James, Roger, Susan, Beverly
Front: Clara and Glenn Larson

San Diego, until his discharge from the Navy in 1976. He then worked as an airline pilot.

Glenn enjoyed sharing his Navy story with friends and family, who were drawn to him, his stories, and his laughter. Unfortunately, he died of a heart attack in 1984. He was buried at Regent, North Dakota, near his parents.

Clara, who turned 97 on May 9, 2021, lives with her daughter, Dorothy and her husband in Indiana, and has continued to provide information toward this story.

AFTERWORD

Clara, Shirley Larson and Bev Christensen inside U-505 in 1972

The *U-505* is now an exhibit at Chicago's Museum of Science and Industry. After the war, it was slated for demolition, but Father John Gallery of Chicago, brother of Captain Daniel Gallery, persuaded the Chicago Museum to save it. The people of Chicago raised $250,000 to help prepare the boat for the tow. The *U-505* left Portsmouth, Virginia, where it was towed up the coast, down the St. Lawrence River and across four of the five Great Lakes to Chicago, a distance of 3000 miles, for installation at the Museum. In 1954, the *U-505* was dedicated as a war memorial and permanent exhibit. In 1989, the *U-505*, as the only Type IX-C boat still in existence, was designated a National Historic Landmark.

For 50 years, the U-boat rested in an outdoor courtyard at the museum in the Chicago elements. In 2004, the museum moved the *U-505* to a new underground, climate-controlled space where visitors are able to see the outside of the sub close up, tour the inside of it, and climb into the re-creation of the crewman's bunk. The 35,000-square-foot exhibit includes an Enigma machine captured from the *U-505*, audio narrative from more than 25 veterans, and 1 of the boat's 2 original periscopes. Millions of people have visited the only German sub in the United States in this exhibit and national war memorial to American sailors. The exhibit area of the "The New *U-505* Experience" includes artifacts and interactive stations to give visitors a taste of what it was like for the crewmen in battle.

I, the author, my husband Steve, my mother Clara, and sister Shirley, first visited the submarine exhibit in 1972, when it was an outdoor exhibit.

My mother and I visited the *U-505* again in 2009, along with Dad's granddaughter, Stephanie, and her husband, Brandon Bratcher. We attended the Task Force 22.3 Reunion, visited with some veterans of the original capture, and toured the *U-505*. I was able to obtain the autograph of several of the original Task Force crew members at the reunion, including Julian Austin.

That evening, my mother and I sat and visited with Don Baker and another member at dinner. The reunion group was served at tables that were set up beside the *U-505*, making it a memorable evening, as stories about the capture were exchanged.

I have compiled the information in this book for posterity, so future generations may better understand this part of the history of World War II, before it is forgotten.

May God bless the past and present veterans who serve to keep America free. And may God bless America, land that we love, so that we may be a blessing to others.

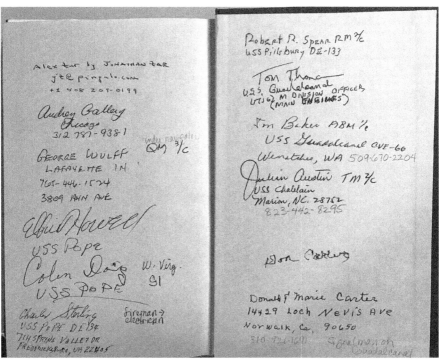

Signatures of veterans that assisted with the capture of U-505 and their families, 2009

REFERENCES

Clara Louise Schweigert Larson, wife of Glenn Peter Larson, Elizabeth, Indiana.

Twenty Million Tons Under the Sea-The Daring Capture of the U-505 by Daniel V. Gallery, published by H. Regnery Co. in 1956, This edition in 2018.

My Navy Career, by Howard D. Sherer,
My Life in the Navy During WWII, December 1, 2009. The memoirs of Howard Sherer, chronicling his life and times on the USS Guadalcanal.

Clear the Decks, by Daniel V. Gallery, New York: Morrow, 1951.

Hunt and Kill- **U-505** *and the U-Boat War in the Atlantic,* edited by Theodore P. Savas, Published by Savas Beatie LLC, New York, NY, 2004.

U-505, by Daniel V. Gallery, 1956, Warner Books, New York, NY

Steel Boats, Iron Hearts - A U-Boat Crewman's Life Aboard **U-505,** by Hans Goebeler with John Vanzo, 2013, Published by Savas Beatie LLC, El Dorado, CA.

The Capture of U-505 - A Legion of Heroes, by Robert McLaughlin, Regent Square Press, Mill Valley, CA, 2017

boat.net, The USS Guadalcanal.

Donald M. Baker, Aviation Boatswain's Mate, 1st Class, USS *Guadalcanal* CVE-60, Task Group 22.3 Association, 2888 Blue Heron Ln, E. Wenatchee WA

U-505, The Final Journey, by James E. Wise Jr., 2005, Naval Institute Press, 291 Wood Road, Annapolis, Maryland 21402, 2005

THE IOWA ENGINEER, October 1942, volume 43, number 1. Member of Engineeering College Magazines Association, Iowa State College, Ames, Iowa

Letter from Becky S. Jordan, Special Collections, 403 Parks Library, Iowa State University, May 7, 2009.

War Training Programs, World War II, Naval Training Schools, Electrical School Information, Ames, Iowa, March 22, 1943.

"The Nautilus" school paper. Published every third week by the U. S. Naval Training School (Electrical-Diesel), Iowa State College, Ames, Iowa, through the Recreation and Welfare Office, 1943.

U.S.S. Guadalcanal Log of Communications, 4 June 1944. www.u- boatarchive. net/U-505-Communications Log.htm

U.S.S. Pillsbury, Commander Escort Division Four, *U.S.S. Chatelain* DE-149 http://www.uboatarchive.net/U-505A/U-505ComCortDiv4Report.htm

Edward Julian Austin, 96 year old veteran of the *Chatalain*, Torpedo Mate, Task Group 22.3, Marion, North Carolina, personal phone calls and correspondence, June 2020.

Wild at Heart, Discovering the Secret of a Man's Soul, by John Eldredge, 2001, Thomas Nelson Publishers, Nashville. **www.ThomasNelson.com**

Saturday Evening Post, *"We Captured a German Sub"*, by Capt. D. V. Gallery, USN, August 4, 1945

THE STORY OF THE U-505, Museum of Science & Industry, Chicago, Illinois, 1955, 1969, 1972
U-505 Capture, aiipowmia.com/inter21/in04260/.htm

U-505, **The Final Journey**, by James E. Wise Jr., Naval Institute Press, Annapolis, Maryland, 2005.

A Quick Flight Back 75 Years, by Penny Rafferty Hamilton, Ph. D., FLY-ND.com. Quarterly, February 08, 2021.

Operation Drumbeat, by Michael Gannon, Harper Perennial, 1991.

The Burning Shore: How Hitler's U-Boats brought World War II to America, by Ed Offley, Basic Books, 2014.

Bev Christensen is a retired Registered Nurse. She has authored articles about community, family histories, pioneer aviators and other writing projects. She has spent the last decade researching and writing *A World War Two Secret*, her new non-fiction book about her father's unique war experience, including the hunt for *U-505*.

Born at Dickinson, North Dakota, Bev grew up on her family's homestead near Regent. She enjoyed swimming and ice skating on Larson Lake and riding horseback with her five siblings. Bev attended a country school for her first two years, and then Regent Public School, which is now the Enchanted Castle Hotel.

During her senior year of high school, she moved with her parents to Eagle Bend, Minnesota, where she graduated. That summer she halter trained foals at a horse ranch near Vining, Minnesota.

Bev attended Dickinson State University's A.D. nursing program, where she met her husband, Steve. She worked as an RN at Long Prairie, Minnesota, Bismarck, and Turtle Lake, North Dakota. She obtained a Bachelor of Science in Nursing from U. of Mary in 1974. That year they took over his family's 1903 homestead near Mercer, North Dakota, where they raised their three sons. Bev spent her last 22 years of nursing in Home Care and Hospice.

In addition to writing, Bev enjoys God's blessings of nine grandchildren, farm life, a couple horses, photography, oil painting, church activities and spending time at Brush Lake with family and friends.

Made in the USA
Middletown, DE
20 June 2022

67326606R00096